THE
WORLDLY
CHURCH

A CALL FOR BIBLICAL RENEWAL

A·C·U
PRESS

C. LEONARD ALLEN
RICHARD T. HUGHES
MICHAEL R. WEED

Book Design, *Mel Ristau*
Cover Design, *Mel Ristau*
Cover Illustration, *Jack Maxwell*

Printed in the United States of America.

Library of Congress Card Number-87-81827
ACU Press, Abilene, Texas
ISBN 0-89112-005-X   *2 3 4 5*

Do not love the world or the things in the world. If any one loves the world, love for the Father is not in him. For all that is in the world, the lust of the flesh and the lust of the eyes and the pride of life, is not of the Father but is of the world. And the world passes away, and the lust of it; but he who does the will of God abides for ever.

I John 2:15-17 (RSV)

Whence comes such vanity in the lives of Christians who enjoy the truth of the Gospel? With what tumults everywhere our lives are filled! We do business, we sail the seas, we engage in wars, we make treaties and we break them, we beget children, enroll heirs, buy fields and sell, cement friendships, erect buildings and tear them down . . . . We are exercised in various arts, sweat and become doctors of law and theology. . . . With such cares we torture ourselves. In this we wax old. In this we let slip so many years and lose that precious treasure which alone is of worth. Then will come the last tribunal where only truth can stand. Too late we shall perceive that all these vanities were but shadows and we have squandered our lives in the delusion of a dream. Some one will say, "Shall a Christian, then, have nothing to do with all of these vanities?" No, not that, but we shall participate only with detachment, being ready to forsake all for the sake of the one thing needful, as Paul said, "Having a wife as if not having," weeping as if not weeping, re-joicing as if not rejoicing, selling as possessing noth-ing, using the world as if not using, for the fashion of this world passes away. Use then the world but delight not in it.

Erasmus of Rotterdam (1466–1536)

For our Children

David, Daniel, and Bethany
Andy
Susan and Jonathan

In Love and Hope

*All scripture citations are from the
Revised Standard Version unless otherwise indicated.*

Contents

Acknowledgments

We are grateful to the following people for reading and commenting upon the manuscript at various stages of its development: Fred Barton, Dallas, Texas; Wendell Broom, B.E. Davis, Carley Dodd, John Robinson, John Stevens, and Gailyn Van Rheenen of Abilene Christian University; Lynn Anderson, pulpit minister of the Highland Church of Christ, Abilene, Texas; Eddie Sharp, pulpit minister of the University Church of Christ, Abilene, Texas; and Jack Reese of the Harding Graduate School of Religion, Memphis, Tennessee. We are especially grateful to Reuel Lemmons, editor of *Image* magazine, Austin, Texas; and William J. Teague, President of Abilene Christian University, for their generous support of this project.

Portions of this book were first presented as lectures and addresses on various occasions, and we express our appreciation for all the encouraging and probing comments we received from those who listened.

Chapter Two of this book reprints with revisions Michael Weed's article, "The Secularization of the Church: From Transcendence to Technique," from the *Faculty Bulletin* of the Institute for Christian Studies in Austin, Texas. We are grateful to the Institute for granting permission to reprint.

Foreword

The secularization of the church has been underway for several centuries now. Ever so slowly secular influence has changed the church. Within the last half century, however, its grip has tightened and it now has the church in a stranglehold. And the church hardly knew what was happening.

If it is not already too late to do much about it, the time at least is short. Religion today is no longer a passion; it is a pastime. Within a single lifetime religion has been reduced to a leisure-time commitment and no longer elicits a conviction of anything sinful.

Typical of the changing church is the fading of the sanctuary and the emergence of the holy gymnasium. Places of worship have become family counseling centers. The turn from prophecy to "need gratification" is producing a modern church that tries to compete in secular gratification with a world that is a master of the art. Someone needs to stay in the soul saving business.

The clash between older Christians and younger Christians is a reflection of the change that is taking place. Older Christians tend to retain some sense of spiritual mission but many Christians in the younger generation seem to consider the church not much more than a social club with a religious flavor.

The role of elders has changed. In ancient Israel, and up to modern times, they were the grizzled greyheads who had learned so much from living that cannot be learned any other way, and who were full of wisdom and compassion. They were role models and counselors. Authority was something they cared little about. But now they are "board members," "directors," and "corporate managers." Now authority is so important that to challenge it is anathema.

The ministry likewise has undergone a profound change. Whereas the preacher once was God's anointed to proclaim the glad tiding of good things, he has become a professional staff manager and counselor. He often is an actor, concerned more with his role, his manners, and his polished delivery than with the possibility of his lips being touched with a live coal from the altar.

The unique quality and ministry of the church is being swallowed up by the secular. We are accentuating the "this-worldly" and depreciating the transcendent. We are turning the transcendent God into an idol—or at least into a servant rather than a master. As a result, we are precipitously close to celebrating a victory of secularism over faith, not a victory of faith over secularism.

Reversing the trend presents a great challenge. Many are giving up faith for secularism. Few are giving up secularism for faith.

This little book sounds the alarm. It questions our infatuation with the fads and techniques of secular modernity. It calls our people back to the worship of a transcendent God and to sacrificial commitment to Jesus Christ as our Savior.

Leonard Allen, Richard Hughes, and Michael Weed issue a call that we all need to hear. They have put their fingers squarely on the most serious challenge facing us today—the secularization of the church. They call us to confront that challenge. They call us back to a sense of the majesty and sovereignty of God, back to a sense of utter dependence upon him, and back to a church living separate and apart from the dominant values of the world.

They do this, not out of disgruntlement or disillusionment, but out of love for the church.

We need to ponder their message deeply. We need to search our souls and rethink our priorities. For it is not necessary that we be popular or successful, but only that we be faithful.

Reuel Lemmons
Editor, *Image*
Austin, Texas

The Identity Crisis of Churches of Christ 1

A missionary, recently returned from foreign fields, approached a congregation of Churches of Christ about support for world missions. The elders were candid. They told him that the concept of world missions no longer has much "market" among Churches of Christ. For this reason, they could not support his request.

Amazed, the missionary asked what the elders considered "marketable" among Churches of Christ today. "Body life," they told him. "Body life."

This story underlines the identity crisis that has become the single most important issue facing Churches of Christ today.

There once was a time when Churches of Christ were widely known as a people of the Book. All who knew us knew that we hungered above all for the word of God. They knew that we immersed ourselves in its truths and sacrificed dearly to share the gospel with those who had never heard. These were our most

fundamental commitments. We knew it, and others
knew it.

But who are we today? What have we become? What is our true identity? What shapes our
world view? What motivates us as a people?

These questions lie at the heart of this book.

We ask them because we fear that the dominant spirit of our secular age has deeply eroded the
biblical commitments of Churches of Christ and sub-
stantially undermined our identity as a people of God.

The pages that follow are rigorous and
make a number of points that may be hard for some to
hear. Some, closely wedded to a secular perspective,
may resent this intrusion into their comfortable world.
Others, having associated a rigorous message with the
hard and ugly sectarian spirit that did incalculable
damage to our movement for so many years, may now
resist a rigorous message of any sort.

From the outset, therefore, the reader
should know the spirit that prompts this book. We
rejoice in the demise of sectarianism among Churches
of Christ. But in far too many instances, sectarianism
has now given way to an easy accommodation to the
values of a secular age. We reject both these postures
and suggest that there is a better way.

That better way is allegiance neither to sect
nor world but rather to a sovereign God who stands in
judgment on both. This book seeks to bring hope and
encouragement, then, to those who are weary of both
sectarianism and secularism and who long for renewal
of biblical faith.

We affirm, first of all, the surpassing truth
that an infinite, transcendent God has brought us redemption from sin and from self. We speak of faith
and grace, of love and service, of the power of God's
Spirit, and of the meaning of the cross.

We seek to reaffirm the great biblical truth that authentic Christianity stems from faith in God, not self; from worship of God, not self; from reliance on God's power, not on the power of self; and from living out Christ's teaching that "whoever seeks to gain his life will lose it, but whoever loses his life will preserve it" (Lk. 17:33, RSV).

These are the themes that must form the identity of Churches of Christ if we are to be taken seriously as a people of God in this world.

The Idea of Transcendence

We have used the term "transcendence" often in this book. By this term we point to the fact that God is infinitely greater than ourselves, that he is the majestic sovereign of the universe upon whom we must depend for life itself, that he works in mysterious ways which often defy our shallow understanding, that he is the very standard of holiness in whose light our noblest efforts are meager indeed, and that we finally must acknowledge his will and not our own.

As several friends and colleagues graciously read the manuscript of this book, several expressed fears that neither the term nor the concept of "transcendence" would communicate with many members of Churches of Christ. If these fears are justified, they point to the very problem we wish to address. For the loss of the sense of a transcendent God is the very heart of the secular perspective. Secularism, after all, insists that there is nothing ultimately mysterious and that, through reason and proper technique, the human mind can understand and even control all that it encounters.

The term "transcendence" or a derivative occasionally appears in Scripture, as for example in 2 Corinthians 4:7: "But we have this treasure in earthen vessels, to show that the transcendent power belongs to God and not to us." The context of this verse illumines the meaning of the concept of transcendence in a powerful way.

Paul has remarked that people whose minds have been blinded by "the god of this world" simply cannot see "the light of the gospel of the glory of Christ, who is the likeness of God" (vss. 3–5). Though Paul may be tempted to change his message to suit those who have been blinded by "the god of this world," he refuses to do so. Instead, he preaches "Jesus Christ as Lord" (vs. 5). After all, "it is *the* God," not the god of this world, who has revealed to us the glories that transcend the frailties of this world.

Put another way, Paul clearly understands that the power and glory of God "transcends" this world and cannot be compromised with the world, its interests, its needs, or its goals.

In addition, the concept of transcendence appears over and again in Scripture apart from the explicit term. Consider, for example, the following passages and what they tell us about the nature of God.

> *To whom then will you liken God,*
> *or what likeness compare with him? . . .*
> *Have you not known? Have you not heard?*
> *Has it not been told you from the beginning?*
> *Have you not understood from the founda-*
> *tions of the earth?*
> *It is he who sits above the circle of the earth,*
> *and its inhabitants are like grasshoppers;*
> *who stretches out the heavens like a curtain,*
> *and spreads them like a tent to dwell in;*
> *who brings princes to nought, and makes the*
> *rulers of the earth as nothing. . . .*
> *Have you not known? Have you not heard?*
> *The Lord is the everlasting God,*
> *the Creator of the ends of the earth.*
> *He does not faint or grow weary,*
> *his understanding is unsearchable.*
> *(Isaiah 40:18, 21–23, 28, RSV)*

Here Scripture speaks of God as the infinite and majestic one, wholly sovereign over the universe. Elsewhere Scripture makes the same point by speaking of the frailty and limited understanding of humankind. Thus, God asks Job,

> *Where were you when I laid the foundation of the earth? Tell me if you have understanding. Who determined its measurements—surely you know! Or who stretched the line upon it? On what were its bases sunk, or who laid its cornerstone . . . ? Have you commanded the morning since your days began? and caused the dawn to know its place . . . ? Have the gates of death been revealed to you, or have you seen the gates of deep darkness? Have you comprehended the expanse of the earth? Declare, if you know all this. (Job 38:4–6, 12, 17–18)*

Hearing all these questions from God, Job of course is forced finally to admit that

> *I have uttered what I did not understand, things too wonderful for me, which I did not know. (Job 42:3)*

The New Testament upholds this point in other ways. At Mars Hill, for example, Paul proclaimed that

> *the God who made the world and everything in it, being Lord of Heaven and earth, does not live in shrines made by man, nor is he served by human hands, as though he needed anything, since he himself gives to all men life and breath and everything. And he made from one every nation of men to live on all the face of the earth, having determined allotted periods and the boundaries of their habitation, that they should seek God, in the hope that they might feel after him and find him.*

Yet he is not far from each one of us, for "In him we live and move and have our being"; as even some of your poets have said, "For we are indeed his offspring." (Acts 17:24–28)

The term "transcendence," then, points to two great biblical themes: the majesty and mystery of an infinite and sovereign God, and the fundamental frailty of humankind whose imperfections and limitations place between God and his creation an enormous gulf.

It is this gulf, however, that the secular spirit of our age denies. Most people living in developed nations today simply assume that little or nothing can defy human understanding and that there is no problem that cannot finally be conquered through reason, science, and technological advancement. The secular spirit sharply diminishes the sense of mystery and the awareness that anything might be above and beyond the powers of human understanding. The notion of God as transcendent becomes an antiquated curiosity—something our ancestors believed but something only fools or weaklings might believe today.

Churches of Christ Today

It is not surprising that this spirit of secularism has invaded Churches of Christ, for we are all active and engaged participants in this modern age. We are bankers, attorneys, physicians, engineers, scientists, and educators. We are psychiatrists, executives of major corporations, real estate developers, investors, politicians, and business people of all sorts. We live and work in a world where the loss of transcendence is widely assumed.

This simple fact about ourselves is central to understanding the problem we face.

Seventy-five years ago, members of Churches of Christ typically came from what the world called "the wrong side of the tracks." Often uneducated, poor, and dispossessed, we had little influence or power either as individuals or as congregations. In those days it was easier to trust in God for we knew our limitations all too well.

But we have changed. Within the last twenty years especially, American members of Churches of Christ have spiraled upward to a much higher socio-economic plane. Now we are educated and often affluent. Many of us wield power in our communities. By virtue of our training and our work, we are often skilled in the arts of management, manipulation, and technique. These very skills subtly promote the loss of a sense of transcendence among us. For if we are accustomed to exercising power and control it becomes more difficult to acknowledge the power and control of a sovereign God.

Another dramatic change has accompanied this socio-economic shift among American Churches of Christ. In the old days we often nurtured a rigid, dogmatic, sectarian spirit and frequently held ourselves aloof from the communities in which we lived. Today, however, that posture of aloofness is largely gone. Instead, we are deeply involved in our communities, serving our neighbors in a myriad of ways. We minister to families and to singles. We reach out to the suffering and the dispossessed. We feed the hungry and cloth the naked. We care for the aged and the infirm and extend compassion and understanding to those who hurt.

We applaud the softening of sectarianism as well as the fact that Churches of Christ today often are deeply involved in serving those around them.

At the same time, we are deeply concerned.

We are concerned because our ministries often seem rooted in the world of self-reliance—the world where so many of us live six days of the week—instead of the world of biblical theology. Put another techniques obscures our identity as children of God.

We sometimes seek to heal marriages, for example, by employing the latest secular therapies instead of the Kingdom values of losing self in serving others, extending grace and forgiveness, and acknowledging the powerful grace of God. Or again, we may seek to enhance family relations in the body of Christ by providing little more than instruction in communication skills. Lessons on good communication would be fully adequate elsewhere, but there is far more to be said about family relations in the context of the body of Christ. The fact that we are children of God has immense implications for our roles as mothers and fathers, sons and daughters, husbands and wives.

Of even greater concern is that, in an increasing number of pulpits of Churches of Christ, preoccupation with meeting contemporary "needs" has all but crowded out biblical theology. Some of our congregations feed far too infrequently on the gospel of Christ. They listen instead to seemingly endless sermons on how to have happy marriages, on how to cope with drugs, and even on how to achieve success in the world. And some church leaders seem convinced that the church will not grow unless people are attracted first by topics of contemporary secular interest. They appear to believe that the gospel, on its own terms, holds little relevance for modern men and women. And sometimes well-meaning Christians actually strip the gospel of its transcendent meaning and reduce it to a formula for success.

All of this is what we mean by secularization of the church. We are concerned that Churches of Christ may slowly and imperceptibly become little more than a social club with religious veneer. We are committed to service and good works, but without the gospel consistently heralded and understood, we may finally differ little in emphasis from the Kiwanis Club, the Rotary Club, or the local PTA.

We quarrel not at all with ministry to families, to the infirm, to the aged, and to the suffering who need our aid, for Christ himself taught us this concern. But the first task of the church is to proclaim the good news that a transcendent God has brought redemption from sin and from self. And the various ministries which claim our time and attention must be rooted deeply, not in secular theories and objectives, but in that very same gospel which is, after all, our only reason for existence.

Looking Ahead

Given the new socio-economic status of Churches of Christ today and the secular world in which so many of us by necessity are immersed, it will be extremely difficult to withstand the secular pressures that surround us. And yet we must do just that. To be an authentic people of God, we must hold to a radically different—and a radically biblical—worldview, one founded upon two pillars. First, we must develop within ourselves a keen sense of the lordship of a God who transcends our poor judgment, our mistaken calculations, and our frail and meager skills. And second, we must understand clearly the subtle nature and power of the secular perspective. We must recognize its allurements and seductions and the inroads it makes into the lives of our congregations.

Such conviction and awareness are essential to recovering our identity as Christian people in the world today. And it is finally this—our identity as Christians and as a community that belongs to God—that this book is all about.

Our first task in this book is to explore the secular perspective and the ways it affects the church. The next chapter therefore examines the meaning of secularism and describes secularized religion in broad and general terms. Chapters three and four then explore the relation of secularization to the history and identity of Churches of Christ.

Finally, chapters four and five hold up a vision of the transcendent God, of the cross of Christ, of the power of the Spirit, of the nature of worship, and of the role of Christian faith in a secular world. Here we suggest that only a renewed commitment to biblical theology can enable Churches of Christ to persist as an authentic people of God.

We pray that this brief volume will be received in the same constructive spirit that prompted its writing, and that it will do abundant good in the fellowship of Churches of Christ.

Secularized Religion in American Culture 2

Before we deal explicitly with Churches of Christ, we need first to describe the meaning of secularization and its effect on religion today.

Nowhere is secularized religion more apparent than in Europe. The visitor there will be struck by the many cathedrals and churches standing in the centers of the great cities, towns, and even the small villages. Their majestic spires tower above surrounding buildings, pointing silently into the sky.

But these monumental structures are largely empty. Today they stand as mute but vivid reminders of the past, examples of medieval architecture, ecclesiastical museums of earlier centuries of Christendom. These empty buildings also bear witness to the fact that European society has undergone a gradual but far-reaching change which has displaced religion from the center of both public and private life.

The complex process whereby this change has come about is commonly referred to as "secularization."[1] In essence this has meant a radical shift in consciousness affecting perspectives on time, history, society, and ultimate reality.[2]

Although the origins of secularization are traced to various sources, most careful observers agree that Western society largely has become a secular civilization.[3] This means that traditional religion no longer plays a central role. More specifically, secularization involves at least two separable dimensions. First, it points to a decline in the importance which society attaches to religious institutions. Second, it signifies an erosion of religious consciousness in the minds and lives of human beings.

For Western civilization this has meant that traditional Judeo-Christian values, beliefs, and aspirations that formerly gave coherence, meaning, and direction to society largely have disappeared from the public arena. In turn, this has resulted in what Richard Neuhaus has aptly labeled "the naked public square," that is, a public arena with no consistent self-understanding or accepted vocabulary, values, and vision to offer cohesion and direction.[4] As a result, modern society no longer depends upon an integrated consensus of values and tends toward becoming an agglomeration loosely held together by modern techniques and procedures.[5] The result is that modern society is an unstable hodgepodge of jarring and clashing ideas (naively called "pluralistic") without shared values and a clear vision of the human good.

Curiously, in America, where religion is apparently healthier, the process of secularization is thought by many to have advanced even further than in Europe.[6] This seeming contradiction—a highly secular society with thriving religious institutions—is generally explained by the fact that secularization has followed different patterns in Europe and America. Whereas in Europe secularization has meant wholesale defection from the church, in the United States it means that although churches and religious institutions tend to thrive, "their specifically religious character has become steadily attenuated."[7]

This means that the churches in the United States have survived by adapting to the pressures and demands of modernity. In so doing, they have insured their survival in the midst of a highly secular society— at least for the immediate future.[8]

Still, this adaptation has cost dearly. It has meant that religion has survived in the United States by radically altering its role and function—in the life both of society and of the individual church member. In short, it has meant the emergence of the "secular church."

As the church adapts to its new role in a society where it is seen as increasingly marginal and in which religion is confined to the private realm, the church undergoes many changes. Utility becomes the guiding principle of the church as it commends itself as useful in the business of life (as well as in the business of business) in terms of society's own standards and values. This basic orientation marks both the organizational structure of the church and the church's understanding of its mission.

On the one hand, the church assumes the characteristics of a technological, bureaucratic, and secular institution. The church thus becomes an assemblage of committees, meetings, questionnaires, memos, copy machines, and related procedures that maintain institutional momentum. On the other hand, the church maintains itself and redefines its mission by seeking to address the endless "needs" of the secular society's casualty list. The cost of life in the secular society is one of failed marriages, soaring abortion rates, crime, delinquency, suicide, drug addiction, nervous stress, mental breakdowns, and the disorientation of our youth.[9]

Thus the secular church alters traditional ministries (e.g., evangelism becomes "outreach") and proliferates a host of new ones through which it seeks to "meet needs," attract outsiders, and involve insiders. The emerging secular church becomes a veritable beehive of busyness. Its members are involved in a swelling number of activities and non-traditional ministries ranging from new member assimilation and stress reduction techniques, through assertiveness training and sensitivity training, to hiking and ski outings.

Since the needs created by modernity's fast pace continually change, the secular church commits itself to monitor the latest shifts and fads which announce the appearance of "new needs." The secular church therefore requires a "market analysis" which can identify "affinity groups" and newly emerging ways by which it can further accommodate itself to society.

In all this, the secular church—changing its offerings and samples in response to the appetites of consumers—more nearly resembles a delicatessen than it resembles its historical namesake. Coherence in the secular church is rarely sought. In fact, it is frequently avoided because it curtails the freedom of expression and diversity demanded in meeting the different needs of a pluralistic society.

Members are exhorted to involvement and sharing and even to serving. Less frequently are they encouraged to discipleship, Bible study, and worship. The context in which all this occurs, therefore, is more nearly that of contemporary self-realization theories than of traditional concepts of salvation.

Clearly, as the self-understanding of the church changes, so does that of those who serve the institution. Not surprisingly, the role of the minister undergoes radical alteration. The traditional role and tasks of the minister as representative of the Christian faith, interpreter of Scripture, teacher of Christian doctrine, and exhorter of the faithful no longer are respected in society and become increasingly irrelevant even within the evolving church.

In order to survive within the secular church, the minister must give special attention to style and technique and develop skills suitable to his changing persona. To paraphrase Bryan Wilson, ministers must now develop new styles and manipulate their images to conform to the expectations of an increasingly secular clientele.[10]

Thus in our bureaucratic, technological, therapeutic, and politicized society, ministers substitute managerial techniques, counseling skills, and—less frequently—political activism for the vital center of Christian faith. In all of this, the modern minister becomes but a reflection, and his voice but an echo, of the secular society he serves. Occasionally the minister achieves "relevance," but it is the relevance of the popular or the so-called prophetic relevance of the popular unpopular.

As the church alters its identity, its self-understanding, and its mission in society, it plays a different role in the life of the average church member. For older church members the secular church retains some of its traditional functions. For younger and newer members, however, the secular church offers no inclusive vision of reality—much less a system of beliefs or doctrines. The religious consciousness of the average church member is an eclectic congestion. For the most part, it consists of a subjective and highly unstable mixture of bits and pieces taken from folk wisdom, horoscopes, "Dear Abby," and the latest version of pop psychology.

Not surprisingly, in the life of the average member of the secular church, the church plays only a marginal role. Secular Christianity is a leisure-time pursuit. The secular church becomes a "Christ Club," providing conviviality, "meaningful personal relationships," occasional intellectual stimulation, recreation—and just enough religion to salve consciences. The church, however, offers no coherent vision of the universe and no moral framework by which one may live.

The Cost of Accommodation

In spite of its apparent successes, accommodation to the methods, procedures, and values of modernity exacts a high price and creates fundamental problems in both practical and theological terms.

On a practical level, the secular church commits itself to provide what the society also provides, in many cases as well as or better than the church. Further, the more successfully the church addresses and gratifies various needs of modern persons (e.g., belonging, self-esteem, meaningful personal relationships, involvement, recreation), the more it legitimates the pursuit of their satisfaction. It is simply a matter of time until many, guided by the pursuit of "need gratification," find their needs more adequately addressed through alternatives such as health spas, service clubs, and the like.

Further, it may be a serious blunder to suppose that the church may be more successful in promoting its message to secular and even hostile audiences by adopting the standards of secular modernity. Secular Christians, like spoiled children, may become more, not less, self-centered and insistent, demanding increasing degrees of attention and accommodation.

A serious question facing the secular church is whether it possesses a faith that can be passed on to future generations. More precisely, is the secular religion merely a good time religion? It remains to be seen whether the secular church can survive and sustain faith in times of struggle and hardship.

It is arguable that the secular church's widespread adoption of the perspectives and methods of secular modernity may bring only apparent and short-lived successes. To the extent that this is true, the secular church represents not the victory of faith over the world but the seduction of the faith by the world's artful techniques.[11] To borrow an image from Peter Berger, the secular church recalls the plight of the drunkard who walked in the gutter to avoid falling off the curb.[12]

The secular church's adaptation to modernity, and particularly its wholesale adoption of the utility principle, leads directly to fundamental theological problems. The most far-reaching of these is a loss of the sense of transcendence.

Ultimately, religious concerns are simply not reducible to nor compatible with methods and techniques based on the assumptions of secular modernity. "Religion necessarily speaks another language, offers itself in different terms and by different criteria, from those that prevail in the technological world of modern society."[13] However innocent the intent, reliance on the utility principle inevitably diminishes and finally eliminates our awareness of transcendence. In a secular world that must quantify, manage, program, and manipulate, the unfathomable mystery and majesty of the biblical God simply does not fit.

Of course, the language of traditional religion and piety still abounds in the secular church. But this language only maintains an illusion—it masks a false transcendence, where

> *religion is put into the service not of gratitude, reverence, and service to God but of human interests, morally both trivial and serious. Religion—its theologies, its cultic practices, its rhetoric, its symbols, its devotions, becomes unwittingly justified for its utility value.*[14]

The result of this process is that "God is denied as God; God becomes an instrument in the service of human beings rather than human beings instruments in the service of God."[15] The loss of transcendence yields a human-centered theology, wherein the human perspective becomes the sole measure and goal of religion.

Not surprisingly, this shift from transcendence to a human perspective defines the secular church's understanding of such activities as worship and such concepts as salvation. Worship becomes a quasi-entertaining event providing an "emotional outlet" and promoting self-esteem and conviviality ("fellowship"), and often lacking reverence, awe, and an awareness of the mystery and majesty of God.

Salvation or redemption necessarily remains an imprecise concept in the secular church, equated loosely with the promotion and gratification of the needs and interests of the self, narrowly defined. Therapeutic terminology may be employed to define God's role in salvation as promoting "self-realization." Regardless of the many variations, however, salvation comes to be understood as attained by and apparently equated with self-indulgence.

Visions of salvation do occasionally extend beyond the boundaries of self-gratification to the broader social and political goals as evidenced in the various "cause theologies" (e.g., black theology, feminist theology, moral majorityism, and liberation theology). As diverse as these different theologies may appear, however, underlying all their differences is a highly selective use of God and biblical motifs to legitimate and promote personal and moral goals. Regardless of one's sympathies, there is little difference between using prayer and piety to achieve personal business success and using prayer at political demonstrations or sit-ins.[16] In both, religion becomes merely a utilitarian value.

Finally, the loss of transcendence and the radical shifts this loss occasions also give rise to additional practical problems of enormous dimensions.

Leaders in the secular church repeatedly will encounter difficulty on occasions when it is necessary to call for humility, patience, and sacrifice. The secular church, built around the promotion of self-esteem, gratification of needs, and self-fulfillment, simply cannot, in any consistent or convincing manner, call for self-discipline, self-restraint, or selflessness. The theology of the cross can have no real place in the "Christ Club."

Recovering the Way

It has always been a difficult task for the church to be in the world and yet not of the world. The secularization of the church is but one more example of that on-going struggle. Whether the church succumbs to the lure of power and prestige or more innocently seeks only a temporary and tactical alliance with modernity, the secularization of the church is a particularly insidious kind of conformity to the world.

This is true for at least two reasons. First, the secular church can point seductively to its many real and tangible successes. Second, the methods of secularism mask themselves as merely neutral tools, no better and no worse than their users and the goals they serve. Yet, hidden assumptions ride in the wake of secular techniques which the church may naively seek to use in managing and promoting "kingdom business."

"Recovering the way" will depend primarily on recognizing the dimensions of the problem. While such recognition must remain partial and incomplete this side of a transcendent perspective, de-secularization of the church is a fundamental task which calls first for recovery of an awareness of transcendence.

By the very nature of the task, however, there can be no formula, much less a technique or strategy, for such a recovery. The very attempt to seek such a solution would in itself be symptomatic of the problem of the secular church, and any such solution would only be another form of false or domesticated transcendence. A true recovery of transcendence cannot be managed, either by traditional piety or by modern techniques. Nor can there be any assurance that a true recovery of transcendence will result in "successful" programs and "efficient" institutions.

An openness to transcendence may begin with a return to the biblical records of God's shattering and unpredictable incursions into human history. Standing alongside Abraham, Moses, or Isaiah, we may encounter God's irreducible "otherness"—the unfathomable mystery and incalculable majesty. Such an awareness may evoke a sense of awe and rekindle near forgotten memories that "his ways are not our ways." It may remind us that God is worshipped not because he is useful, but because he is God; that he is not the guarantor of our hopes for something else, but he himself is the ultimate goal of all our hopes.

Only such an encounter with the God above our countless gods can release us from self-entrapment within a web of human-centered illusions and fantasies. Only such an awareness can expose and restrain the bloating human ego, swollen by countless forms of self-delusion. An openness to the Transcendent One will occasion an awareness of our own sinfulness and our rebellion against our Creator, Judge, and Redeemer. We will confess with Isaiah:

> *Woe is me! For I am lost; for I am a man of unclean lips, and I dwell in the midst of a people of unclean lips; for my eyes have seen the King, the Lord of hosts! (Isaiah 6:5)*

It is only through such an encounter that we can perceive our true nature and destiny.

Such a vision is critical if the church is to make any meaningful and faithful attempt at "meeting needs." It is only in this attitude that the church may recognize and redirect false needs and identify secondary ones idolatrously masquerading in the guise of ultimacy. Only from this perspective can it be grasped that true human freedom is freedom-in-limitation and that true human dignity is that which reflects the character and purpose of the Transcendent One.

For the Christian this character is given its fullest expression in the Incarnation, not as a "celebration of humanity" nor as a sanction of human ambitions, but culminating in the uncalculating selflessness of the cross. For the church, the community of the cross, this rich symbol must remain at the center of worship and life as a constant reminder of who we are and as a guide to who we are called to be. When Christians forget who they are and who they are called to be, no amount of technique or programming will restore lost integrity.

The church does not simply need more experts in communication, counseling, or church growth. It does not need more leaders who are clever and successful. But it desperately needs more leaders who are wise and faithful to the crucified one. Wise leaders will challenge the near equation of cleverness with wisdom and of successfulness with faithfulness. Idolizing success not only can be countered, it must be countered. While a faithful church may be a successful one, a successful church is not necessarily a faithful one.

Wise and faithful leaders will do well to listen to an old German proverb: "He who marries the spirit of the age soon becomes a widower."

---

[1]The term "secularization" originally designated the removal of land from ecclesiastical control in sixteenth-century Germany. In sociological theory it designates a lessening of the significance of religious institutions and beliefs in society. Secularization as a modern social phenomenon is generally linked to the advance of industrialization and technology. While it has a distinctive shape and unique interaction with features of Western

civilization, it is by no means confined to the West and in fact may be detected in Eastern cultures subject to the impact of modernity. Cf. Peter Berger, "Secularity, West and East," *This World* (Winter 1983):49–62.

[2]For a succinct and insightful assessment of key components of modern secular consciousness, see Peter Berger, "Toward a Critique of Modernity," in *Facing up to Modernity* (New York: Harper & Row, 1977), pp. 70–80.

[3]It should be noted that there are many different versions of secularization theory. These differ regarding such matters as the origins of secularization, whether it is evolutionary or cyclical, and whether it is confined to the West or global.

[4]See Richard John Neuhaus, *The Naked Public Square: Religion and Democracy in America* (Grand Rapids: Eerdmans, 1984).

[5]Bryan Wilson, *Contemporary Transformations of Religion* (Oxford: Clarendon, 1976), p. 102.

[6]Bryan Wilson, *Religion in Secular Society: A Sociological Comment* (Middlesex: Penguin Books, 1969). "Superficially, . . . and in contrast to the evidence from Europe, the United States manifest a high degree of religious activity. And yet, on this evidence, no one is prepared to suggest that America is other than a secularized country. By all sorts of other indicators it might be argued that the United States is a country in which instrumental values, rational procedures and technical methods have gone furthest, and the country in which the sense of the sacred, the sense of the sanctity of life, and deep religiosity are most conspicuously absent. The travellers of the past who commented on the apparent extensiveness of Church membership, rarely omitted to say that they found religion in America to be very superficial. Sociologists generally hold that the dominant values of American society are not religious" (p. 112). For the debate on this issue, see Gary S. Smith, "The Great Secularization Debate in America," *Reformed Journal 35* (July 1985):15–19.

[7]Bryan Wilson, *Religion in Sociological Perspective* (New York: Oxford, 1982), p. 152.

[8]*Ibid.*, p. 174.

[9]Wilson, *Religion in Secular Society*, p. 94.

[10]Wilson, *Contemporary Transformations of Religion*, p. 91.

[11]*Ibid.*, p. 86.

[12]Peter Berger, "A Sociological View of the Secularization of Theology," in *Facing up to Modernity*, p. 178.

[13]Wilson, *Religion in Sociological Perspective*, p. 45.

¹⁴James Gustafson, *Ethics From a Theocentric Perspective* (Chicago: University of Chicago, 1981), 1:25.

¹⁵*Ibid.*

¹⁶*Ibid.*, pp. 22, 23.

The Secular Church in the Restoration Movement 3

As the previous chapter pointed out, the notion of secularization points to the loss of a sense of transcendence in our lives. And no sensitive Christian today can fail to be aware that this loss has captured vast segments of American Christianity. For many television preachers the biblical question, "Is it true?" has given way to the pragmatic questions, "Will it work? Will it pay? Will it sell?" And some shamelessly erode the claims of Jesus Christ beyond all recognition in their efforts to "market" the Christian faith.

Logically, the end of secularization is outright atheism where God is simply not considered. But as we have seen, a far more subtle form of secularization prevails in many of America's churches. Here, God is alive, but not well. He has been tamed, domesticated, and put to work in the service of human objectives.

Instead of hearing his call to holiness, we call on him for peace of mind. Instead of hearing his call to suffering servanthood, we call on him for divine assistance in our own pursuit of health, wealth, and success. Instead of hearing his call to worship, we call on him for enhancement of self-esteem. In all this, we shape the agenda and set the terms. He is merely the Great Assistant in the Sky who aids us on our self-chosen way.

In this chapter, we want to be more precise about the origins of secularization and the roots of the secular world view. How has it happened that American Christianity has been so thoroughly seduced by a perspective so alien to the Christian faith?

But beyond this, we want to ask some tough questions about those of us in the heritage of the Restoration Movement. Has secularization affected only the television preachers and the mainstream denominations? What about ourselves? Is secularization at work among Churches of Christ as well? And if so, to what extent? These questions we dare not ignore.

Once before we ignored a process so visibly at work in much of American Protestantism and claimed it could never happen to us. That process was the tragic division that afflicted Baptists, Methodists, Presbyterians, and other groups before and during the Civil War. We claimed we could never divide, for we were the New Testament church. But even in the midst of these claims, division was implicit in our ranks and by 1906, division was apparent even to the census takers of the United States government.

Today we face a potential crisis of even greater magnitude: the crisis of secularization. It is easy enough to believe that because we are the primitive church, we are immune to the trends of the modern world. We will suggest, however, that such naive beliefs constitute an open invitation to secularization to invade the church and subvert it from within. This may be the single most important issue facing the church in our time. But it goes barely recognized and largely undiscussed by church leaders or by individual Christians.

What, then, are the sources of secularization in our modern world?

*The Roots of
Secularization*

Secularization has deep roots in the eighteenth century, the age of the Enlightenment.[1] In the seventeenth century, science burst on the western world with new discoveries, new insights, new techniques and new methods for improving the life of humankind. If men and women in previous epochs had been totally dependent on God for life and health, by the eighteenth century it became clear that human beings could enhance and even extend their lives through their own rational and scientific efforts. The power, the mystery, and the sovereignty of God over human affairs began to recede as women and men placed increasing trust in their own ability to manage their own affairs and determine their own destiny.

One can measure in two ways the profound impact this perspective exerted on American Christianity. First, revivalism and evangelism underwent a significant transformation. In the Great Awakening of the early eighteenth century, Jonathan Edwards could stand amazed at what he called "the surprising work of God" in his time. Who could measure or predict the movings of God's Spirit, and who could withstand the power of his sovereign grace? God, in Edwards' view, stood beyond prediction and manipulation. Instead, he was simply GOD, the transcendent Lord of the universe who moved in mysterious ways to work his gracious will.

By the early nineteenth century, however, this outlook had changed. Charles Finney, the greatest revivalist of Alexander Campbell's day, was not content to wait upon "the surprising work of God." Instead, as a true child of the Enlightenment, he undertook to "manage" the revivals and manipulate God's grace with what he called his "new measures." He instituted "inquiry sessions" and the "anxious bench" where he focused public attention on convicted sinners. He launched the "protracted meeting" to manipulate sinners to respond to the call of God. And he employed a small army of assistants to work the neighborhoods and turn out the crowds.

If Edwards' revivals had been the work of God, Finney's revivals were the work of the man and his assistants. Edwards' "surprising work of God" had given way by the nineteenth century to rational technique and manipulative management.

One can also measure the impact of the Enlightenment on the Christian faith by the shift in millennial thinking in that age. Prior to the eighteenth century, those who expected an earthly millennium commonly thought it would come only at God's instigation. Human beings were too wicked and helpless to bring about such a momentous event for themselves. They could only wait on Christ's coming when God himself, at his own pleasure and initiative, would launch the millennial reign. We recognize this view, of course, as premillennialism.

But in the eighteenth century, men and women increasingly believed that they themselves had the power, through science, technology, and the progress of civilization, to launch the millennial dawn. From this perspective, God became increasingly irrelevant. The millennium would be a human creation, a product of rationality, management, and technique.

From that time until this, the faith of western men and women in their own abilities to enhance and even perfect human life on this earth has grown by leaps and bounds. In the process, God slowly has faded into irrelevance in many western nations.

As we observed in chapter two, the hollow and empty European cathedrals mutely testify to this development. There, secularization has proceeded in a straightforward and logical way. God simply is not a serious option for the vast majority of Europeans. For most, life is lived entirely on a horizontal plane. The vertical dimension is largely gone, an awareness of transcendence has largely disappeared, and human beings themselves reign sovereign over human affairs.

In America, however, the secularization of religion has taken a circuitous route. Many American churches, afraid of extinction and concerned with survival in this modern world, have adopted the old saw, "If you can't whip 'em, join 'em." Ironically, they have therefore embraced the very perspectives and techniques of secularization itself.

In the first place, their concern to survive led American churches to concern themselves primarily with success, with numerical growth, and with outward progress. This in itself was a significant concession to the values of the culture, for the call of the gospel is for faithfulness, not for success. At the same time, it was this concession that undergirded all other concessions. For in their zeal to "succeed," the churches often abandoned the mandate to faithfulness and committed themselves to meeting a whole host of "needs" that were not connected with the gospel in any fundamental way.

We must underscore here what was said in the previous chapter concerning the church's rush to "meet needs." When "meeting contemporary needs" is divorced from biblical theology in the life of the church, the church has given up one of its most precious possessions: its identity. When this occurs the church has essentially become like a business, monitoring the marketplace, assessing the fads, and determining what will appeal in a given season of a given year.

This utilitarian concern for "meeting needs" has operated in American Christianity to some extent for nearly three centuries, and churches have paid a heavy price for this commitment. Indeed, they paid most dearly in their sacrifice of biblical theology.

One of the earliest "needs" to capture the attention of American Christians was the "need" to defend God against the onslaughts of the rationalists and secularists in the eighteenth and nineteenth centuries. Ironically, those defenders of the faith employed for this purpose the very assumptions of the rationalists they opposed. Armed with reason and logical proofs, they rushed to prove God's existence in scientifically irrefutable ways.

When they had finished, the infinite, transcendent, and sovereign God of the universe had all but disappeared. What was left was little more than the end product of a syllogism, void of mystery and power. This rational, demonstrable, and proven "god" was not the infinite and transcendent God of Abraham, Isaac, and Jacob, but a domesticated and manageable god for a secular church in a secular age.[2]

If the eighteenth and nineteenth centuries sacrificed a sovereign and transcendent God on the altar of "meeting needs," the twentieth-century church has sacrificed on that same altar the biblical notions of sin and salvation. Our secular civilization argues that human beings are not inherently sinful or broken or alienated from God, but only flawed in minor ways. What they need, therefore, is not salvation from sin, but rather counseling and therapy—a quick fix to repair the damage and put them back on track.

By the mid-twentieth century, this assumption was prevalent in American culture, and Americans turned more to secular therapists than to preachers for mental and spiritual healing. When this occurred, the churches rushed to employ therapists and counselors of their own.[3] In the process, many congregations slowly and subtly redefined their mission. By the waning years of the twentieth century, many American churches seemed more concerned to save marriages than souls, more interested in self-esteem than salvation, and more concerned to relieve depression and anxiety than to deal with the fundamental reality of sin.

Secularization in American Christianity, then, confuses the sacred and the profane, domesticates God, eradicates a sense of sin, reduces salvation to self esteem, and trivializes the Christian faith. It rivets God so completely to the earth that little remains that is holy, transcendent or sacred.

In effect, God becomes our agent who does our bidding, pleads our case, reduces our anxieties, heightens our self-esteem, and aids us on our self-chosen path to worldly success. Secular Christians thereby abandon the vertical dimension between God and humankind. The horizontal dimension alone remains, and God becomes merely one object among other objects in a horizontal world, awaiting manipulation by secular Christians in a secular church.

But what does any of this have to do with our own Restoration Movement? Simply this: Churches of Christ are also susceptible to the forces of secularization. This is true for at least three reasons, all rooted in the history and nature of our movement.

Secularization in the Restoration Movement

The Sectarian Perspective. First, there is a close connection between sectarianism and secularization. By sectarian, we mean the belief that the church has been fully restored by our forebearers, that the American Churches of Christ are fully identical to the primitive churches in every significant respect, and that there is now nothing left to do but defend the gains of the past. Surely this spirit has characterized many in our movement.

The naivete of this position makes its proponents especially susceptible to secularization. The sectarian mind, after all, is unaware of the enormous extent to which culture moulds lives, shapes faith, and even helps determine the concerns of the church in every age.

The power of culture is unavoidable. Like death and taxes, it is one of those things from which we cannot escape. It is part and parcel of being human, of having limits. Our task, therefore, is to heighten our awareness of culture's power in our lives, for only when we become alert to culture's seductions can we do battle with its principalities and powers, unmask its pretentions, and reject its idolatrous claims. To do otherwise is to invite our culture to control our faith and to shape the church in ways we might never intend.

This, however, is precisely the risk the sectarian Christian takes. He assumes that the church in which he lives has been fully restored, when in fact it may reflect his own cultural interests to a far greater extent than he is aware.

The American church historian, Henry Bowden, recently pointed to this very tendency in many restoration movements. Having surveyed the histories of many groups who sought to recover the church of the apostolic age, he drew this conclusion:

> *One is reminded of George Tyrell's observation about New Testament scholars of last century who limited their view of Jesus to an incarnation of their own ideals. They could find only a German in the Jew, he said, a professor in the prophet, the nineteenth century in the first. The Christ identified by such a narrow search, looking down through centuries of Catholic darkness, produced only the reflection of a Protestant face at the bottom of a deep well. This appears to be the case with restorationists, too.*[4]

Bowden's judgment clearly applies to restorationists who claim they have completed their course and finished their search. For the search is never fully done. Paul, himself, was quick to admit that he had not arrived. "I press on," he wrote, "toward the goal for the prize of the upward call of God in Christ Jesus." (Phil. 3:12–14)

Restoration must be conceived as ongoing process, not as final achievement, a process which takes seriously the fact of sin and the pervasive reality of finitude in our lives. Restoration is valid only when grounded in the conviction that we fall short even in our noblest efforts and best intentions, that we therefore stand under the judgment of God every hour of every day, and that we are finally saved by the grace of a sovereign and transcendent God and not by our own works—including our own success in restoring the primitive church.

The alternative to these admissions is to kid ourselves into believing that we are in control of the world in which we live. The alternative, in fact, is to pull God from his throne and to enthrone ourselves instead. Ironically, both sectarians and secularists alike delude themselves with precisely these assumptions, for both believe that perfection lies within their reach if only they can muster sufficient grit and self-reliance.

It is important to recognize that the sectarian and the secularist, at least in this respect, share a common worldview. When individual Christians take a sectarian stance, therefore, it may be a short and easy step to secularization. In the first place, the path has been paved with common assumptions. And in the second place, Christians who despair of the bondage of sectarianism may later find themselves in the secularist camp simply because they have never developed a truly biblical worldview on which to build a meaningful alternative.

The Enlightenment: Seedbed of Our Movement. The second reason Churches of Christ are especially susceptible to secularization has to do with our early history in the nineteenth century. The critical fact in this regard is that our movement was born of the same intellectual currents that launched the process of secularization in the eighteenth century, namely, the Enlightenment. Virtually all the leaders of our movement in the early nineteenth century—and especially the Campbells—had been nurtured in Enlightenment thought and sought to apply the insights of that perspective to religion. Their objective was the unity of all Christians and, in keeping with their age, they devised a rational plan whereby this objective could be accomplished. That plan was simply this: "If we restore the primitive church, then Christians will be united."

Historian Samuel S. Hill has commented suggestively on the "if . . . then" approach to religion employed by the Campbells. Strikingly, he describes their approach as a "'modern' or 'liberal' avenue of access to God." In keeping with the spirit of the Enlightenment,

> *spiritual achievements [here became] regular, predictable, and logical. . . . Mystery and a trusting providentialism had yielded to common sense, to* quid-pro-quo *reasoning, to certain kinds of rationalistic, mechanical thinking.*[5]

The extent to which the Campbells reflected the Enlightenment is also apparent in their contention that restoring the primitive church not only would bring unity; it also would hasten the millennial dawn. This was no premillennialism which waited for God to institute his golden age. Rather, their vision was an Enlightenment-informed postmillennialism according to which they themselves were major actors, hastening history toward its final end.

Since the Campbells, our movement has been deeply informed by the spirit of the Enlightenment. Often, we have nurtured a kind of boot-straps religion, a sort of spiritual self-reliance, very much in keeping with the larger American culture. We have sometimes called this posture "legalism," but self-reliance by whatever name is self-reliance still.

We have preached too little over the years of the frailty, the finitude, and the shortcomings of humankind. We have preached too little of the transcendence, the sovereignty, the grace, and the love of God. Too often we have preoccupied ourselves with the human response, with what humans must do to secure their own salvation, with exhortations to duty and faithfulness, and with admonitions to keep the law of Christ. Too often we have assumed that human beings are fully capable of keeping the law and dispatching their duty. Too rarely have we considered that we are frail, finite, and broken and stand in the most desperate need of the unmerited grace of God.

F. L. Rowe once told of an evangelist revered among Churches of Christ who held a gospel meeting in Cincinnati in the late 1930s. Rowe confided in a private letter that this evangelist "preached four very forceful sermons, largely pugnacious, and I asked him at the supper table to preach a sermon on the Prodigal Son. He hesitated a minute and then said, 'Brother Rowe, I cannot do it, I never have studied that subject.'"[6] This incident symbolizes well the extent to which Churches of Christ in those years neglected the themes of grace and love, and preached instead a rigorous and demanding gospel of duty, self-reliance, and law.

So what might all this say of secularization? Here is the point: the very heart and soul of secularization is self-reliance. From the secularist's perspective, humanity will achieve its own goals with its own resources in its own good time. We wonder: if for 150 years we often have neglected both the finitude of humankind and God's transcendence and grace, and if the message we have preached has focused on self-reliance, then what resources do we now possess to withstand the forces of secularization working in our midst today? Can we point to an infinite God and, trusting him, reject the pretentions of our culture? Or are we more likely to incorporate those pretentions into our corporate faith, sanctify them, and carry on?

The Modern Context. The third reason Churches of Christ are especially susceptible to secularization has to do with our very recent past. In the 1960s, the traditional values of our culture were questioned on all hands. Not surprisingly, the traditional formulations of the Restoration Movement received serious scrutiny as well, and many found the tradition of self-help, the emphasis on legalism, and the entire rational heritage of the Enlightenment to be sorely lacking. In the midst of this examination, some of those left Churches of Christ altogether.

Among those who stayed, however, many discovered for the first time the great themes of God's sovereignty, transcendence, and grace. The heavy emphasis on the Acts of the Apostles diminished, Romans and Galatians became open books, and many pulpits virtually rang with the good news of salvation for frail and miserable sinners.

The good news of salvation, however, was not the only show in town. A competing attraction was the good news of self-esteem, at least in some of our churches. In this, we but followed the lead once again of the culture in which we lived. The leaders in this case were evangelicals who in the 1950s discovered the usefulness of popular psychology and put it to work—they thought—in the service of the faith.

Popular psychology became by the 1960s and 1970s, however, the tail that wagged the dog. For many evangelicals, happiness in this present world overshadowed life in the Spirit and comfort in the here and now displaced salvation from sin. Biblical theology often took second place to "Christian psychology" by which happiness and comfort might be achieved. David Harrington Watt, a historian of American evangelicalism, writes that

*in the 1960s and 1970s evangelical maga-
zines often seemed to be little more than self-
help compendiums.Evangelical bookstores were
full of books that treated subjects such as family relations, alcoholism, old age and death,...
Evangelical readers were told "how to fight
depression and win," and offered "God's Rx
for Depression." They were told how to be calm
and content and how to avoid fatigue. They
were advised to "help [themselves] to happiness;" they were told "how to live in heaven on
earth."[7]*

In those same years, pulpits here and there among Churches of Christ adopted many of these themes. By the 1980s, these concerns had become standard fare in many of our congregations, in various periodicals circulating among Churches of Christ, and especially in national media presentations.

The transition from the arid, rational legal-ism of the first half of the twentieth century to obses-sion with self-esteem, family relations, and conquering depression in more recent years can easily be ex-plained. In the first place, the evangelical preoccupa-tion with healthy and productive living in the here and now seemed to many people in Churches of Christ a positive alternative to the negativism, the sectarian divisiveness, the debating, and the argumentative spirit that often had dominated the church's past. In this regard, the adoption of the evangelicals' agenda had much in common with the discovery of grace: both were positive, hopeful, and encouraging.

In the second place, Churches of Christ were competing with evangelicals in the vast, free mar-ket of souls. And we were fundamentally concerned that people come to our churches, not elsewhere. It was simply a matter, therefore, of surviving through meeting needs. It was apparent that debating and logi-cal discourses were not producing the growth we sought. But the topics of family, anxiety, mental health, and self-esteem seemed likely hooks by which people at least could be attracted to Churches of Christ. While, in theory, presentation of the gospel would come later, that presentation in actual practice often never occurred.

Finally, the pop psychology gospel of the evangelicals seemed strangely comfortable—almost like an old shoe—and it wore so well and felt so good that many were reluctant to slip it off. The fact is, it *did* fit. It fit because it was, at its core, the old nineteenth-century gospel of self-reliance in new and modern garb.

The gospel of psychology, with its emphasis on family relations and self-enhancement, was itself an offspring of the eighteenth-century Enlightenment. Like the Enlightenment, it valued the individual, self-help, and human progress—themes which Churches of Christ have prized for 150 years. Further, for those members of Churches of Christ who had never really heard or never understood the message of God's sovereignty and grace, the secular gospel of the evangelicals was appealing, indeed. Again, the road from sectarianism to secularism is paved with common assumptions, and for many who became disenchanted with sectarianism in the 1960s and the 1970s, that road was a natural and easy one to take.

The Secular Church Today

Today secularization is clearly at the gates of Churches of Christ and, in some instances, well within the city walls. One hardly could find irony and paradox set in more striking relief. How is it that a church which claims to model itself after primitive Christianity, which prizes ancient norms and apostolic practices, which prides itself on being a people of the Book— how is it that the Churches of Christ, in these waning years of the twentieth century, can be so thoroughly at home in this modern, secular world?

As we have seen, the forces of secularization did not arrive yesterday or the day before. Instead, while our brotherhood concerned itself with defending the old paths against liberalism and then humanism, secularization stalked our blind side. It seduced us when we were least aware. Ironically, we often succumbed to its seductions in our own well-meaning attempts to expand the borders of the kingdom.

What evidence do we find for secularization in our congregations today? Reuel Lemmons suggestively wrote,

> *Jesus said we should be the salt of the earth.*
> *[But] I see very few salty churches....*
> *We have drawn so heavily upon our culture...*
> *that there is little about us that is unique except in our own eyes.*[8]

Lemmons is right.

We see evidence of secularization, first of all, in congregations whose first concern in evangelism and edification is to gauge the market place and meet current needs.

We see evidence of secularization in congregations more concerned with growth and numerical success than with preaching the gospel in its purity and simplicity.

We see evidence of secularization when we hear church leaders speak of "making churches grow," as if they were the ones to give the increase.

We see evidence of secularization when we hear church leaders seriously defend the construction of exercise facilities and basketball courts as absolutely essential to evangelism, as if God could not work apart from these facilities.

We see evidence of secularization when we hear ministers, who should know better, contend that the church cannot reach the lost in this modern age through serious Bible study but only through "meeting needs," as if the Word of God alone is impotent. Thus, they defend as central to evangelism such classes as "Coping with Anxiety," "Dealing with Drugs," "Building Better Families," "Planning for Retirement," and "Building Self Esteem."

We see evidence of secularization in the educational programs of many congregations where serious study of the Bible has taken second place to these very same themes.

And we see evidence of secularization when elders candidly admit that missions is no longer "marketable" among Churches of Christ whose chief interest, they contend, is "body life."

Clearly, the first order of business for any congregation of Christ is to proclaim the sovereignty of God, the sinfulness of humankind, and salvation through the grace of Jesus Christ. Congregations which allow aerobics, marriage therapy, counseling centers, and self-enhancement fads to preempt this first concern simply have lost their way.

Our concern over these matters does not arise because someone, somewhere, is failing to conform to a particular biblical pattern or blueprint. In fact, our concern has nothing to do with issues such as this at all.

Rather, we are concerned because these developments often reflect a spirit of self-reliance, a dependence on fads and trends and the spirit of the age rather than on the power of the cross at work in our lives.

*The Task of
Ministry*

At this point, we need to be very clear regarding the entire question of practical "helping" ministries.

In the first place, many practical ministries do abundant good in the lives of people, and no one can fail to rejoice when good is done.

At the same time, it is possible for practical ministries to stand in direct opposition to the cross of Christ. This can happen in at least two ways. First, ministries concerned with self-esteem often have as their chief objective the enhancement of the human ego and the nourishment of human pride. Such objectives stand diametrically at odds with the cross of Christ which calls us to lose ourselves for the sake of others, not to find ourselves through the power of self-esteem. It must be said, therefore, that self-esteem born of self-sufficiency is fundamentally unchristian and finally even counter-productive. On the other hand, confidence in my redemption based on an awareness that the Sovereign Power of the Universe has accepted me is a confidence that will never die.

Second, ministry opposes the cross of Christ when a minister assumes that, through his various techniques and therapies, he can bring about healing, put his "client" back on track, and finally judge his efforts in that particular case a resounding success.

Such assumptions grossly underestimate the power of sin and the depths of alienation and estrangement in the lives of every human being. Any minister who aims for some kind of final "success" has grounded his ministry in a profound illusion. The very best for which any family minister or counselor can ever hope is for partial and fragmentary success and for short term gains. For after we have done all we know to do, the power of sin remains.

What we must always remember is that our various ministerial techniques can focus only on the outward symptoms—failed marriages, depression, drug addiction, and estranged relationships of all kinds. The real disease—pride, greed, self-interest—remains always and ever beyond the reach of our pitifully impotent methods, techniques, and therapies.

But precisely here we come to the crux of the matter of practical ministry. Secular counselors and therapists understandably direct their work only toward the symptoms of the human condition. Many secular therapists, in fact, may confuse the symptoms with the disease and assume that they are addressing, through their various techniques, the real and ultimate problem in a given situation. For this reason, they often indulge themselves in the illusion of success.

Christian ministers, however, if they make any legitimate claim to representing the cross of Christ, can indulge themselves in no such illusion. They must recognize always the problem behind the immediate problem, the question behind the immediate question, the dilemma behind the immediate dilemma. And they must recognize with clear vision that the ultimate problem is one that, so long as this life shall last, will never go away.

But there is more. The ultimate problem—the problem of sin and alienation—is precisely what points us to the Ultimate Answer. And it is here that the work of the Christian minister differs profoundly from the work of the secular therapist. The Christian minister may indeed address the various symptoms of alienation—failed marriages, disrupted families, and other similar problems. But let him not think that, in doing this, he is performing the fundamental task of the Christian minister. All of this the secular servant does as well.

The Christian minister, instead, addresses the ultimate problem of sin and alienation with the Ultimate Answer: the gospel of Jesus Christ. He never deceives himself into believing that his work is done or that he has achieved success when he has contributed, in some small way, to saving a marriage from divorce, a teenager from the power of alcohol, or an extended family from broken relations. In truth, his work is never done, for sin always remains.

When we indulge ourselves in illusions and deceptions in this regard, we furnish powerful testimony to the fact that we have not really grasped the biblical teaching on sin. We often have thought that sin is a mere violation of the law or a missing of the mark, as if perhaps we miss the mark on one day but hit the mark on three successive days thereafter. But to view sin as a mere violation of the law is foreign to the Bible.

The New Testament teaches that sin is pervasive and lies at the very heart of being human. Paul describes the power of sin in Romans 3:10–18:

> *None is righteous, no, not one; no one understands, no one seeks for God. All have turned aside, together they have gone wrong; no one does good, not even one. Their throat is an open grave, they use their tongues to deceive. The venom of asps is under their lips. Their mouth is full of curses and bitterness. Their feet are swift to shed blood, in their paths are ruin and misery, and the way of peace they do not know. There is no fear of God before their eyes.*

If one thinks that Paul is here describing some people who perhaps are worse than others, or worse than others in certain ways, then he misses the point entirely. Paul here describes something common to the human race: pride, self-interest, and greed—in a word, sin.

It is for this reason that Paul heaps scorn on the notion that one might save herself through works of the law. He makes this point, in fact, with utmost clarity, insisting that "all who rely on works of the law are under a curse." And why? Simply because to save one's self by the law requires keeping all the law—every jot and every tittle. And who among us is capable of such righteousness? (Gal. 3:10–11)

The Christian minister, therefore, must take sin with utmost seriousness. Here, indeed, is the ultimate question: how can I escape the pervasive power of sin? The answer to which this question always points is the Ultimate Answer: Jesus Christ, the Son of the Living God.

If Paul poses the ultimate question in his categorical declaration that "none is righteous, no, not one," he speaks of the Ultimate Answer in Ephesians 2:8–10:

> *For by grace you have been saved through faith; and this is not your own doing, it is the gift of God—not because of works, lest any man should boast. For we are his workmanship, created in Christ Jesus for good works, which God prepared beforehand, that we should walk in them.*

The task of the Christian minister, therefore, is a far deeper and richer task than mere counseling or therapy or moral guidance. His real task—and the far more difficult task—is to lead those with whom he works to see the ultimate question that lies behind the present crisis and the ultimate need that lies behind the penultimate need of the moment. If he is able to do that, he will also be able to point those with whom he works to the Ultimate Answer, God at work in Jesus Christ.

Through all of this, the minister should also see—and keep clearly in mind—that his work as counselor is, by itself, always penultimate. Indeed, so long as he is content to be a mere counselor, specializing in techniques through which he imagines he will achieve "success," so long as he rests content in that objective, he has not yet begun to engage in *Christian* ministry. Only when he takes seriously the pervasive reality of sin, leads those with whom he works to see this reality in their lives, and then points to the Ultimate Word in that situation—only then has he begun to do a Christian work.

This also means that preaching must be the heart and soul of every local church. The fundamental task of preaching is to convict our hearts of the ultimate problem and then to proclaim, in the midst of the crisis of conviction, the Ultimate Answer who alone can heal the power of sin. Further, this unique task of preaching must inform the work of all our practical, "helping" ministries if these ministries are to rise above the level of the merely secular.

Often, however, the influence works the other way around. Instead of the pulpit, with its uniquely Christian task, setting the agenda of the "helping" ministries, the therapeutic and technical aspects of the "helping" ministries often set the agenda for the pulpit.

How does this happen? Perhaps it results from our infatuation with numerical success. What the people really want, we tell ourselves, is family ministry, youth ministry, involvement ministries, and short-term solutions to anxiety and depression. And at one level they do. But instead of leading people to see the ultimate answer behind their immediate needs and then proclaiming the cross of Christ as the Answer of Answers, our preaching often falls victim to the illusion that secondary, penultimate, and "felt" needs are the truly fundamental needs that we must address.

In this way, many pulpits among Churches of Christ have sacrificed proclamation of the cross for proclamation of advice on achieving self-gratification and success in this world.

Other pulpits, in the interest of popular "appeal," downplay the tragedy of sin and suffering and seek to remove from the assembly any sense of estrangement, alienation, or the tragic dimension of life. People live with suffering, tragedy, and ambiguity during the week, the thinking seems to run, and therefore want only an upbeat, positive experience on Sunday morning.

But to refuse to speak of sin, suffering, and the ambiguities of life in our Sunday worship is to evict from our midst the very cross of Christ. To evict the tragic from our corporate life together is to evict the ultimate question upon which hearing the Ultimate Answer finally depends. Without conviction of sin, failure, and finitude, there can be no meaningful sense of grace.

The gospel, after all, proclaims a Christ who entered the earth in a lowly manger, who shared the suffering of humankind, and who finally was nailed to a tree. The gospel is the message of life in the form of death, power in the garb of weakness, and success in the guise of failure.

These, however, are precisely the themes the secular church does not want to hear. Its passion, instead, is for life in the form of life, power in the form of power, and success in the form of success; as a result, it thrusts talk of death, weakness, and failure out of doors. Not surprisingly, then, it confuses immediate, penultimate questions with the ultimate question and its own temporal answers with the Final Answer found in the Crucified One.

Someone at this point is certain to object: "These fellows just don't understand the way churches grow. They don't understand the needs and desires of the people in my community."

We wonder, however, whether one who speaks in this way has really grasped the meaning of the power of sin, on the one hand, and the power of the cross, on the other. And if he has, then what about priorities: is he more concerned for outward success and spiraling growth or is he first concerned with proclaiming the Answer that lies above all the answers devised by human beings?

The church is not called simply to meet needs. It is called, rather, to meet the *ultimate* need. To do less than this is to forget both who and Whose we are and to fail in our calling altogether.

In our zeal for the "practical ministry" of meeting needs, however, we easily forget our ultimate calling and identity and lose sight of the biblical base for all that we are and do. When this happens—and it happens with increasing regularity—many Christians often view the church as little more than a civic club with religious overtones.

In this context, we often *behave* like a civic club with religious overtones. Is it any wonder, for , example, that one current trend in building programs is to hire financial consultants from outside the congregation who teach us how to orchestrate a secularly-based "fund raising campaign" in the body of Christ? Is it any wonder that our children in the body of Christ exclude one another from groups because of labels on their clothes or the high schools they attend? Is it any wonder that adultery and divorce run at near epidemic proportions in many congregations? And is it any wonder that evangelism is a low priority item for many members of Churches of Christ?

If we lose sight of our biblical identity and offer to the world only basketball and aerobics, counseling and therapy, and sound techniques for building better families and enhancing self-esteem, then we really offer very little that is not provided already by capable experts in fully secular settings. And more important, we have not even begun to engage ourselves in authentic Christian ministry.

To find our way back home, we must begin with what we have always urged through the years, namely, a return to the Bible. The solution must run deeper than this, however, for we first must reject the notion that the Bible is a manual for self-help or for do-it-yourself-righteousness. Such a view of Scripture will only compound our problem. Instead, we must hear in the Bible that voice of God who exposes our

The Way Back Home

sin, who leaves us undone, and who finally points us to himself as the only source of righteousness and salvation.

We need to hear in our current malaise the words of Job whose encounter with God unmasked his pretentions and led him to exclaim,

> *"I had heard of thee by the hearing of the ear,
> but now my eye sees thee; therefore I despise
> myself, and repent in dust and ashes."
> (42:5-6)*

When we have truly accepted our frailty and acknowledged our unfaithfulness, we must then hear the glorious words of Paul which proclaim redemption and salvation even in the midst of our failures.

> *...in all these things we are more than conquerors through him who loved us. For I am
> sure that neither death, nor life, nor angels,
> nor principalities, nor things present, nor
> things to come, nor powers, nor height, nor
> depth, nor any thing else in all creation, will
> be able to separate us from the love of God in
> Christ Jesus our Lord. (Rom. 8:37–39)*

This is the gospel of the Lord Jesus Christ. It is this, and this alone, that enriches and enlarges the flock of Christ and gives us all a place to stand.

In the chapters that follow, we explore more fully the nature of secularization, its presence among Churches of Christ today, and—more important— answers to the question: What can we do about it?

[1]On the Enlightenment and its impact, see G.R. Cragg, *From Puritanism to the Age of Reason* (Cambridge: Cambridge University, 1950), and Henry F. May, *The Enlightenment in America* (New York: Oxford University, 1976).

[2]See James Turner, *Without God, Without Creed: The Origins of Unbelief in America* (Baltimore: Johns Hopkins, 1985).

[3]For an indepth treatment of this shift, see E. Brooks Holifield, *A History of Pastoral Care in America* (Nashville: Abingdon, 1983), esp. pp. 259–306.

[4]Henry W. Bowden, "Perplexity Over a Protean Principle: A Response," in *The American Quest for the Primitive Church*, ed. Richard T. Hughes (Urbana, IL: University of Illinois, 1988).

[5]Samuel S. Hill, "Comparing Three Approaches to Restoration: A Response," in *The American Quest for the Primitive Church*.

[6]Letter in Abilene Christian University Archives.

[7]David Harrington Watt, "Evangelicals and Modern Psychology," paper read at the American Society of Church History meeting, Chicago, IL, December 1986.

[8]Reuel Lemmons, "Community Should be Aware of Church," *Christian Chronicle* (January 1987):19.

The Scandal of the Gospel Today 4

The heart of early Christian preaching was "Jesus Christ and him crucified" (1 Cor. 2:2). The apostles proclaimed that God had accepted death in the form of a crucified Jewish manual laborer from Galilee. They proclaimed that he had done this in order to break the power of death and bring salvation to all people. And when they proclaimed such a message, it appeared as nothing less than scandal to people across the Roman world. Paul wrote:

> For the word of the cross is folly to those who are perishing, but to us who are being saved it is the power of God . . . . For Jews demand signs and Greeks seek wisdom, but we preach Christ crucified, a stumblingblock [scandal] to Jews and folly to Gentiles.
> (1 Cor. 1:18, 22–23)

Today, the "scandal" of the message remains.

The message of the cross remains a scandal not only to the world at large but even to the church itself. The church always has been about the business of softening the sting of its message, of removing the scandal from the cross. For the church seeks to be popular, to claim the powerful and the respectable among its holy ranks. It seeks—because it is always in part a human church—to be in step with the times. It seeks this mostly out of sincere concern to lift up the fallen, to bless those who feel cursed, and to help relieve the burdens of the guilty and hurting. But somewhere the scandal, the offense, gets blunted.

We find ourselves telling the world what it wants to hear instead of what it needs to hear. And often we tell ourselves the same things. The gulf between the holiness of God and the sinfulness of human beings narrows. As we have seen, the things that matter most to the world often set the agenda for the church. In virtually every age, those who call themselves the church gradually take on the shape and color of the culture, enshrining its idols, sanctifying its values, and blunting the scandal of the cross.

What is that scandal today? What is the offense of the cross in our age? In one sense, the offense today is just what it always has been. For the cross points to a God who identifies most closely with the weak and suffering, a God who calls people to deny self, to serve instead of being served, and to confess their hardheartedness. The cross points to a God who promises that somehow through all of this, through losing our lives, we will find them. The offense, Paul said, is "Christ nailed to the cross" (1 Cor. 2:2, NEB).

But do we really know what this means for the Churches of Christ in America in the late twentieth century. What is the scandal today, for us?

To focus that question, we must look further at the pervasive secularism of our time and its more modern roots. As we have seen, the term "secularization" points to the notion that this world is all there is—or at least all that matters. And while the Enlightenment gave rise to this notion in the eighteenth century, two later developments gave it tremendous support.

The first of these developments was the theory of evolution popularized by Charles Darwin. It must be said that Darwin was simply a scientist who also viewed himself as a faithful member of the Church of England and had no intention of ridding the universe of God. Nonetheless, his view of "natural selection" did tend to undermine the traditional view of the world as designed by God and sustained by divine providence. Many people after Darwin came to view life on earth as little more than a cruel process of survival within a mindless system. In a Darwinian universe, as commonly conceived, humanity was on its own from conception to grave. For many, God simply became an anachronism.[1]

In the early twentieth century, Sigmund Freud, with his psychoanalytical theories, furnished the second strong support for a secularized worldview. Freud concluded that our esteemed rational powers, through which we define values and derive meaning, are not as rational or objective as people like to think. Rather, they are merely marching to the tune played by dark, uncharted instincts buried deep within our subconscious minds.[2]

The impact of these complex developments in our time has been immense. In Western culture the result has been the widespread sense that God is elusive or perhaps not there at all, that the heavens above are closed, and that human beings therefore are thrown back upon their own resources. Therefore, if meaning or fulfillment or happiness is to be found, it will be found, not by appeal to a shadowy God, but only within human beings themselves.

To live in a secular world is to live in a world where many people sense that the heavens are fastened shut, where God is not involved and will not reach down, and where human beings in the final analysis must achieve their own salvation. In this world there is a sharply diminished sense of overarching, invisible realities surrounding daily life and giving it meaning. The world, rather, is just as it appears: nothing more and nothing less. We live in such a culture today, a culture considerably different from that of the first-century Jew or Greek.

The grave problem is simply this: while secularism shapes our culture, it also changes the face and message of the church. Such a development is not surprising, for in some form it has happened to the church in almost every age of its existence. Yet, the apparent blindness to what is happening and the scarcity of protesting voices should concern us all.

Members of Churches of Christ have prided themselves on being "first-century Christians," a people who scorn human traditions and cultural norms, but we must face the stark fact that we are often more the product of our times and of our traditions than we have imagined. We are not just "New Testament Christians"; we are also very much twentieth-century Christians. And we cannot simply assume an easy correspondence between the two.

To understand where we are today, we must look again—in even more depth and detail than we did in chapter three—at the profound cultural changes that occurred in America in the 1960s. In that decade, a new locus of authority emerged. Many questioned or rejected the authority of traditional values and turned instead to the "self" as a new authority for a new age.

This shift had profound implications for the church. Until that time many viewed the church as an institution that *set standards* for society. But in the 1960s they began to view it more as an institution that *met the needs* of society. Many churches, therefore, began shifting their emphasis to meet the new expectations. They shifted their emphasis from God's demands to people's wants or needs. They downplayed distinctive Christian teachings and equated being Christian with being "truly human." "With the self as the author of authority," one historian observed, "one's feelings became the ultimate criterion for everything. Indeed, even the church became a place where people went to feel good about themselves."[3] For many people, psychology became the ruling discipline in all realms of life, and in such an atmosphere there soon emerged what has been termed a "therapeutic Christianity."[4] Those with eyes to see could observe, especially among liberal churches, a sharp trend toward cultural accomodation and a corresponding loss of a clear biblical message.

Conservative or evangelical Protestants sharply criticized such trends. Evangelical leaders castigated liberals for their easy embrace of the spirit of the times and their undermining of biblical authority.

As we have moved into the 1970s and now the 1980s, however, an irony has emerged: evangelicals have followed in the footsteps of the very liberals they once rebuked, especially in their growing "subjectivization" of the Christian message. Like the liberals of the 1960s, evangelicals became preoccupied with self-fulfillment, "psychological balance," and a sort of Christian hedonism.[5]

Though in theory still affirming a high view of the Bible, evangelicals embraced the spirit of the age with nearly as much ardor as did the liberals of the 1960s. As a result, they increasingly redefined theological terms by psychological or sociological concepts, making the faith more human-centered and less God-centered. Finally, they commended the faith more for its usefulness than for its truth. In short, those who claimed to uphold conservative orthodoxy had secularized the faith.

For us in Churches of Christ the point simply is this: we may consider ourselves distinct and separate from these conservative Protestants, but the same cultural forces that shaped them are shaping us as well. We, too, partake deeply of the secular spirit of the age and often gear our message to the utilitarian demands of our time.

How is it possible that this can happen among Churches of Christ today?

The Rationalization of Faith

In chapter three we noted that the Enlightenment exerted a profound influence on our movement in its early years. The restoration fathers laid out a pragmatic and utilitarian approach to the Christian faith which we described as an "if . . . then" agenda. "If we restore the primitive church," our forefathers surmised, "then we will hasten both the unity of all Christians and the millennial dawn." The initiative here was not God's, it was their's. And the burden of transforming the world lay heavily upon them as God's agents in the latter days.

Now we want to see how the Enlightenment helped shape two other important dimensions of our movement: our doctrine of the Holy Spirit and our view of the Bible.

To understand the impact of the Enlightenment on our view of the Holy Spirit, we must remember that in that vaunted age the supremacy of human reason and progress rendered God more and more an afterthought. Indeed, many felt that he merely had created the universe, laid down its laws of operation, and then stepped back to let it run itself. In this milieu, God was not involved in the lives of human beings and his very existence became increasingly a matter of rationally verified propositions. The result was "a severely stripped down version of Christianity, with all that smacked of mystery and superstition pared away."[6]

Although Alexander Campbell and other early leaders resisted such radical forms of Enlightened religion, this trend shaped their thought extensively. After all, John Locke (1632–1704), one of the most influential proponents of a rational Christianity, was Campbell's favorite philosopher.[7] Steeped in the Lockean perspective, Campbell rationalized the doctrine of the Spirit, stressing that in conversion the Spirit worked only through the clear and rational language of the Bible. Campbell did not mean to deny that the Spirit could work in people's lives "without the Bible, and without words." But his rational emphasis heavily overshadowed the direct and personal dimension of the Spirit's work. And as a result, many of the preachers who allied themselves with Campbell virtually banished the Spirit as the living presence and power of God in this world.[8]

Campbell, for example, could argue that "if the Spirit of God has spoken all its arguments" in the Bible, then "all the power of the Holy Spirit which can operate on the human mind is spent." And Walter Scott, the great evangelist, stated that the work of the Spirit was not to "enter the soul of the sinner" but rather to convince "us as we convince one another—by truth and argument."[9] Here was a secularized doctrine of the Spirit, a doctrine in which God's power and presence in this world was sharply restricted.

Under such influence Churches of Christ developed and sustained a theology of self-reliance. For if God indeed had withdrawn to the heavens, leaving behind merely arguments and laws to direct human lives, then clearly the burden fell upon human understanding and performance.

The Enlightenment also exerted a profound impact on our understanding of the Bible. Many members of Churches of Christ today, while viewing the Bible as inspired, still think the Bible essentially a book of good common sense or even sound psychological theory. They assume that the Bible, like any good self-help manual, contains straightforward formulas and workable techniques that any intelligent person will find sensible and reasonable. In this view, faith involves little that is mysterious or beyond one's understanding—nothing much more than deep down common sense and the willingness to practice some new personal enrichment techniques. As a result, many believers find, perhaps to their surprise, that God's ways are indeed very much like their own.

What is the source for this peculiar understanding of the Bible? Again, we turn to the Enlightenment. Our forefathers—men like Campbell, Tolbert Fanning, and J. W. McGarvey—adopted a way of reading the Bible called the "inductive method."[10] The Bible, in this view, was a grand collection of individual "facts." The task of the Bible student became simply that of collecting the scattered facts and classifying them according to topics or doctrines. He might use a concordance to pull together many of the verses where a particular word was used. The resulting sermons and writings nearly always were topical, constructed out of dozens of passages drawn almost indiscriminately from across the wide range of biblical literature. With such a method, they thought, the Bible did not require interpretation. One simply gathered and set forth the "facts." Thus, Tolbert Fanning could write that "all the sacred records contradict the supposition that an interpreter is needed."[11]

This way of reading the Bible became a powerful tradition among Churches of Christ—an especially subtle one, we might add, since our forefathers often claimed to allow no human traditions to shape their reading of the Bible. And it brought problems. For with this method the New Testament became essentially a law book or divine constitution for the church, with most of the doctrinal "facts" reduced to a level of equal importance. The Bible became atomized, broken up into separate little bits of doctrine which could be codified into law. It became a document filled with workable formulas, neat blueprints, a document above all eminently rational and suited, many thought, to the new scientific ways of knowing.

The consequences of such a view were far-reaching. The focus began to fall heavily on obeying the laws, building by the blueprint, working the formulas, and knowing all the right "facts," in short, upon human knowledge and performance. Salvation came more and more to rest upon the proper functioning of the human brain. God, of course, had done his part long ago and it now remained only for human beings to engage their minds, dig in their heels, and bring the plan to completion.

Such a method of reading the Bible made it very difficult to distinguish the "weightier matters" from the less weighty ones, the central doctrines of the Bible from subordinate ones. Scripture, we might say, became "flat," that is, all its "facts" and commands became of "first importance." Christian identity and salvation came to depend on getting them all right, or at least the ones we judged to be "binding." Often enough, the result has been rancorous debate, division, and abiding animosity over what is central or peripheral, essential or nonessential.

Today many in Churches of Christ have moved away from this way of reading the Bible. Some, however, have done little more than exchange the old common sense approach, with its mechanical tones, for a new and more marketable version of the same thing. They have exchanged one self-help formula for another.

In such an exchange the losses outweigh the gains. For our traditional way of reading Scripture, even with its shortcomings, always exalted the text and took it with utmost seriousness. But today that appears to be less and less the case. Today the demand for quick answers, slick formulas, entertainment, and instant gratification of "needs" make it increasingly difficult for churches to sustain serious Bible study.

Certainly at one level the Bible can be read as a common sense book. Many of its truths can pass the tests of logic. Its wise sayings do indeed reflect the way life seems to work. And a good bit of its advice appears to make for what we would call good psychological health. But none of this constitutes the heart of the Christian gospel. The tests of rationality, common sense, or psychological health also certify the message of an Eric Fromm (*The Art of Loving*) or a Leo Buscaglia (*Loving Each Other*)—men who make little or no claim to be Christian at all.

We do not have to reject the common sense dimension of Scripture or celebrate the irrational, but we cannot let such messages, even in Christian guise, masquerade as the good news of Jesus Christ. For the gospel concerns something very different from all of this. It is about the heavens being opened and God coming down. It is about God in his love and mercy doing what we in our weakness and sin could never do for ourselves. It is about a God who "is able to do far more abundantly than all we ask or think" (Eph. 3:20).

Consequences

As a direct result of these eighteenth and nineteenth-century backgrounds, with their emphasis on self-reliance, three significant trends point today to the impact of secularization among Churches of Christ. First is the emergence of what can be called a prudential gospel, that is, a gospel proclaiming Christ as a mere means to an end. As secularism advances, people increasingly focus on the utility value of their faith, on its ability to meet an ever-increasing array of subjective human needs. Faith in God increasingly becomes little more than a useful tool for people to employ as they seek to fulfill their potential and reach their own goals.

Nowhere can this tendency be seen more clearly than in how we answer the central question of evangelism, "Why become a Christian?" In our churches today that question receives ever more pragmatic and selfish answers. We hear of marriages thriving, of businesses prospering, of treasure ships coming in. We hear of what Christ will do for our sex life and for our faltering ego. We hear how biblical principles will give a person the worldly success he seeks. What we do not hear so much is the far more central answer. "Why become a Christian?" Because it is true. "Why become a Christian?" Because God through Christ has atoned for our sin and called us in love to take up the cross in his service.

What we often miss is the paradox of the gospel, the scandal of the cross. The call of Christ is not to personal success and peace of mind, but to brokenness, suffering, and service. Neal Plantinga put it well: "We are intended to please *God*—not the other way around—and the idea that Christianity is something we adopt for what it will pay us in happiness and personal mastery is an idea which must be explicitly discouraged."[12]

A closely related trend revealing the impact of secularism on the church is an excessive focus on the "self." Again, this focus comes as no surprise, given our traditional view of the Holy Spirit. For if God through his Spirit is not an active power in this world, then we are left only with a self-help religion. This traditional focus has been intensified, however, by the therapeutic mindset that became dominant in the 1960s. Since that time, Christians have turned increasingly inward, seeking the personal enhancement that they imagine the gospel will provide. Christian self-help manuals have proliferated, almost keeping pace with their secular counterparts. From the pulpit, even in Churches of Christ, biblical texts more and more have become pretexts for nice little lessons on how to cope with the pressures we bring upon ourselves through our ambitions and our affluence.

With this turn to the self has come, inevitably, a corresponding redefinition of sin and salvation. In the Bible sin is basically a theological concept, that is, it has meaning only in reference to God and his will. But under the impact of secularism, sin becomes merely a psychological concept. We begin to speak not so much of sinful behavior as of unhealthy, neurotic, or repressive behavior. Popular preachers redefine sin as low self-esteem and insist that the Christian life is a divinely sanctioned "ego-trip" and that pride is a virtue and humility a vice.[13] In less blatant forms such views appear to underlie a great deal of what we are hearing in our churches today. Sin is out, self-help is in.

Precisely at this point we are confronted with the "scandal" or "stumblingblock" of the gospel. The gospel is scandalous precisely because human beings inevitably seek to inflate themselves and to glorify themselves rather than God. The scandal of the gospel is the call to bear the cross, to deny and give up ourselves. It is not that we are freed by Christ to love ourselves but rather that we are freed from self-obsession. By heeding his call we are enabled to forget ourselves and to focus our attention upon God and upon those around us who are in need. As Karl Barth put it, the greatest freedom we can experience as Christians is freedom from the self.

A third trend pointing to the impact of secularism today is our widespread reverence for power, control, and wealth. One of the great enemies of the Christian faith in modern times was the German philosopher Friedrich Nietzsche (d. 1900). Nietzsche believed that the essence of humanity consisted in what he called the "will to power." He believed that human beings possessed an innate drive to wield power and to dominate others. By this means—by the sheer "will to power"—one could achieve self-mastery and help forge a future in which people could live entirely without God.[14]

It was for this reason that Nietzsche came to scorn Christianity. He scorned it, we suggest, because he came to understand the scandal of the cross all too clearly. For he saw that Jesus taught his followers to give up their wealth to feed the poor, to sacrifice themselves in service to the weak and dispossessed. He saw that Jesus called people to empty themselves of power and to identify themselves with the lowly. To Nietzsche, this was despicable. Christians exerted far too much energy, he thought, trying to preserve all the weaklings and the wretched of the earth. Such people should be left to perish, and thus to make way for the strong and the heroic.

Today, we need to hear what Nietzsche heard and to see what Nietzsche saw. For though Nietzsche opposed Christianity vehemently, he nonetheless understood clearly the call of Jesus and the meaning of the cross. He understood the Christian view of God's infinite concern for the weak, the poor, and the oppressed of this earth. He found it disgusting, to be sure, but he understood it.

In fact, he may have understood it better than many Christians. For Christianity has now become a dominant cultural force, able to throw its weight around. Christians have learned to admire power, to wield power, and to play power games. We are easily tempted, even in the name of Christ, to dominate others and manipulate them to our own ends. We have learned that wealth means power and that poverty means powerlessness. We have learned that power means success and victory and that weakness means failure and defeat. We have learned to hide our weaknesses and to exaggerate our strengths. And we have learned to despise the weak and admire only the strong.

The trends we have examined—the emergence of a prudential gospel, the turn to the self, and the reverence for power and wealth—point clearly to the deep inroads of secularism among us. When measured by Scripture and much of the great preaching throughout the centuries we can see an astounding shift today. For much contemporary preaching ascribes to humankind the power and glory that belong only to God.

Notice the contrasts. Scripture stresses the seriousness of sin and the need to give up self and the world for Christ. But today more and more we hear people promised the world if they accept Christ.

In Scripture the Christian's most valued victories are over worldly aspirations. But in much contemporary preaching, the most valued victories are over worldly frustrations.

Scripture views pride with its godlike pretensions as the center and source of human sin. But much preaching today roots sin in low self-esteem or the failure to think highly enough of one's self.

Scripture asserts that a person's greatest need is atonement to God, but the secular church proclaims his greatest need as therapy.

Scripture portrays people as afflicted with guilt which only God can relieve. But in a secular environment there are only "guilt complexes" to be exorcised by counselors.

Something terribly vital to the Christian message is lost when therapeutic language crowds out the biblical language of sin and atonement. Further, something terribly vital is lost when a "cash and carry" Christianity replaces a cross-centered Christianity. Something vital is lost when a common sense gospel replaces the powerful and transforming word of the cross.

Paul said that the gospel as he knew it was an offense and scandal to the cultured people of his day. He said it was a message that did not fit with Jewish experience or make sense to the Greek worldview. But what is the scandal of the gospel today in the secular West? What is the scandal in a technologically sophisticated and affluent America? What is the scandal among evangelical churches? What is the scandal among Churches of Christ?

The scandal of the gospel today is that the gospel speaks only of a God-made person, while our culture glorifies the self-made person. The scandal today is the gospel call to surrender self, to offer self to God and his service, when the world calls only for self-enhancement. The scandal is that the heavens are open; that the sovereign God comes to rule this world and all who live therein; that salvation is by divine power, not human achievement or technique. The scandal is that we must be confronted with the depths of human evil and deceit before we can know the heights of grace.

Can we proclaim such a scandalous message today? Can we ourselves even hear it? Can we live in a secular environment and, with Paul, decide "to know nothing but Jesus Christ and him crucified"? Can our pulpits ring with that message? Or must we become an outpost of the secular church? Must we too trade our spiritual birthright for a mess of secular pottage?

To the degree that we close the heavens from our lives and lose a sense of the power of God's Spirit in this world, to that degree we will become little more than a secular church. We may very well pride ourselves on having an orthodox or traditional "form of religion" but if we allow secularity to undermine its substance, we will have lost its transcendent power.

Notes

[1] See Owen Chadwick, *The Secularization of the European Mind in the Nineteenth Century* (Cambridge, 1975), pp. 161–188. The continuing impact of such views can be seen in the title of a recent, well-publicized book entitled, *The Blind Watchmaker: Why the Evidence of Evolution Reveals a Universe Without Design* (New York: Norton, 1986), by Richard Dawkins.

[2] See Hans Küng, *Freud and the Problem of God* (New Haven: Yale, 1978), pp. 31–52.

[3] Leonard I. Sweet, "The 1960s: The Crises of Liberal Christianity," in *Evangelicalism and Modern America,* ed. George M. Marsden (Grand Rapids: Eerdmans, 1984), pp. 31, 38.

[4] See Philip Rieff, *The Triumph of the Therapeutic* (New York: Harper & Row, 1966), and Robert N. Bellah, et.al., *Habits of the Heart: Individualism and Commitment in American Life* (New York: Harper & Row, 1986), pp. 113–141.

[5] James D. Hunter, *American Evangelicalism: Conservative Religion and the Quandary of Modernity* (New Brunswick, NJ: Rutgers, 1983), pp. 84–97; Hunter, *Evangelicalism: The Coming Generation* (Chicago: University of Chicago, 1987), pp. 64–71.

[6] James Turner, "Enlightenment and Belief, 1690–1790," in *Without God, Without Creed: The Origins of Unbelief in America* (Baltimore: Johns Hopkins, 1985), p. 52.

[7] See especially Locke's work, *The Reasonableness of Christianity,* ed. I.T. Ramsey (Stanford: Stanford, 1958).

[8] *A Debate between Rev. A. Campbell and Rev. N.L. Rice on Christian Baptism* (Lexington, KY, 1844), p. 641. See also Thomas H. Olbricht, "Alexander Campbell's View of the Holy Spirit," *Restoration Quarterly 6* (First Quarter, 1962):1–11.

[9] Alexander Campbell, *Christianity Restored* (Bethany, VA, 1835), p. 350; Walter Scott, *A Discourse on the Holy Spirit* (Bethany, VA, 1831), pp. 20–21.

[10] See Michael W. Casey, "The Development of Necessary Inference in the Hermeneutics of the Disciples of Christ/Churches of Christ" (Ph.D. diss., University of Pittsburgh, 1986). For use of the "inductive method" in the broader American context, see T. Dwight Bozeman, *Protestants in an Age of Science: The Baconian Ideal in Antebellum American Religious Thought* (Chapel Hill: University of North Carolina, 1977).

[11] Tolbert Fanning, *True Method of Searching the Scriptures* (reprint ed., Nashville: Gospel Advocate, 1911), pp. 18–21.

[12] Cited in Dennis Voskuil, "The Theology of Self-Esteem: An Analysis," in *Your Better Self: Christianity, Psychology, and Self-Esteem,* ed., Craig W. Ellison (New York: Harper & Row, 1983), p. 56.

¹³Robert Schuller, *Self-Esteem: The New Reformation* (Waco: Word, 1982), pp. 67, 74, 99. For a theological assessment of Schuller's "Possibility Thinking," see Dennis Voskuil, *Mountains into Goldmines: Robert Schuller and the Gospel of Success* (Grand Rapids: Eerdmans, 1983). See also David G. Myers, *The Inflated Self: Human Illusions and the Biblical Call to Hope* (New York: Seabury, 1980).

¹⁴Friedrich Nietzsche, *The Will to Power*, ed. by Walter Kaufmann (New York, 1966).

Recovering the Way 5

When once we discern the forces of secularization at work in the church today, how should we respond? When we see that the "scandal" of the cross has been covered up, how do we recover its transcendent and transforming power? As we pointed out in chapter two, we first must recognize that there is no prepackaged formula or sure-fire technique for achieving such a recovery. Indeed, the very expectation that such a formula might be found betrays the secular categories in which we have grown accustomed to thinking.

Instead, we will have to resist the secular passion for technique, manipulation, and rational control. The God of Abraham, Isaac, and Jacob is not subject to our manipulation. He is a God, rather, whose ways are past tracing out, who dwells in awesome majesty and impenetrable mystery. He works in surprising ways, shattering our vaunted human wisdom, dethroning the lesser gods we create, and choosing the weak and lowly of this earth as his most powerful agents. We can discover no sure formulas to harness his power. However, we can retrace his mighty workings revealed in Scripture and then stand before him with our lives and our churches open to his mighty work within us.

To do that, of course, we must give renewed attention to Scripture. One of the great strengths of our heritage has been the persistent call to take the Bible seriously, to struggle with Scripture afresh in every generation. That is precisely the call we must heed today as we are faced with an ever more secular church. In heeding that call we must not hesitate to call into question, if need be, the way we traditionally have read the Bible. For our task is not merely to preserve the ways of the recent past, no matter how highly we may esteem them, but rather to let God, through Scripture, confront us anew.

Our primary response to the secularization of the church, therefore, must be serious and prolonged engagement with the theology of the Bible. By this we mean the attempt to discern the central, overarching themes of Scripture, those things "of first importance" (I Cor. 15:3). Faced with the vast and diverse body of biblical writings, the discipline of biblical theology seeks to keep before us the central events and formative experiences that mark God's relationship with his people throughout the ages. It seeks to throw into bold relief those basic truths that, through all the twists and turns and ups and downs of biblical history, formed the heart and soul of God's revelation.[1]

This task may seem simple at first, but it is not clear that we are ready to carry it out. For traditionally we have read the Bible in a very different way, a way that has sometimes obscured the great theological turning points of Scripture. It is always difficult to face our weakness, to confront an all-too-human tradition. But there is no reason to deny it, nor any reason to despair in the face of it. It is only when we confront our own finitude and weakness, after all, that we truly can hear the good news of the gospel. It is through facing up to our humanness in such ways as this that we can assume a more attentive posture toward Scripture and let God work more powerfully in our lives.

We must see more clearly that Scripture is not so much an ancient text that we can master with carefully refined study techniques as it is an ancient text through which God seeks to master us. We must read it submissively, in the frailty of mind and body, and thereby experience again and again the life-giving and transforming power of God. An admirer once said to Adolf Schlatter, the renowned New Testament scholar of an earlier day, that he always had wanted to meet a theologian like him who stood firmly upon the Word of God. "Thank you," Schlatter replied. "But I don't stand *upon* the Word of God; I stand *under* it." Here, the preposition matters immensely. We stand under the Word, under a holy and gracious God, allowing him, at every moment, to correct our often blurred and nearsighted attempts to see into his truth.

The secular self-help heresies of our time can be addressed only from this posture—only from a recognition of our frailty, need, and creatureliness. They can be addressed, furthermore, only as we proclaim from our pulpits the great themes of Scripture: the sovereignty and glory of God, the debilitating sin of each person, the searching and suffering love of the Father, the incarnation and atoning death of the Son, salvation by grace through faith, and the transforming power of the Spirit at work within us. These themes mark the highpoints of Scripture and form the very heart of the Christian message. Through the centuries the church has enjoyed its greatest health when it has placed these themes at the very core of its being and proclaimed them with clarity and conviction.

To do this today, we will have to labor long and hard at the discipline of biblical theology. We must not continue, as in the past, simply lining up doctrinal planks of equal size and nailing them into a flat doctrinal platform. Nor, disillusioned with that, can we simply ransack the Bible for those texts that seem most useful for "meeting needs." Rather, we must attempt to discern the theological centers of Scripture, God's decisive and mighty deeds that give everything else its significance and shape.

A Community of the Cross

For Paul that center clearly is the cross and resurrection of Christ. For him, that event is not simply one doctrine among others. Rather, the cross and resurrection form the very fulcrum of faith, the energizing center of relationship with God. Thus he writes:

> *For what I received I passed on to you as of first importance: that Christ died for our sins according to the Scriptures, that he was buried, that he was raised on the third day according to the Scriptures, and that he appeared to Peter, then to the Twelve.*
> *(I Cor. 15:3–5)*

Or again: "I decided to know nothing among you except Jesus Christ and him crucified" (I Cor. 2:2). The core of Paul's preaching was Jesus' cross and resurrection as God's way of dealing with sin. Paul sees Christ's cross and resurrection as one interlocking event, as a single story in which neither aspect can be understood in isolation. In this single event, God's power in weakness is revealed.

Paul describes this central event most often with paradoxical terms. He speaks of death/life, humiliation/exaltation, shame/glory, defeat/victory, of being baptized into death/of being raised into life.

Why this array of paradoxes? Why are death and life, defeat and victory, cross and resurrection always linked? Simply for this reason: Paul knows that God fulfills his promises and works his purposes through suffering, that his victories are won only through weakness, shame, death, and apparent defeat. He knows that God works in ways utterly unlike the workings of human beings.

Precisely here lies the "scandal" of the cross. God reveals his power in weakness and through sacrifice—and not just in any sacrifice, but rather in the shameful, scandalous, "utterly vile" death of his Son on the cross. Martin Hengel, surveying the literature about crucifixion in antiquity, documents in detail just how loathsome an act crucifixion was to the people of the Greek and Roman world. He concludes that "when Paul talks of the 'folly' of the message of the crucified Jesus he is not therefore speaking in riddles or using abstract cipher. He is expressing the harsh experience of his missionary preaching and the offense it causes."[2]

With such a harsh experience, Paul may have wished to downplay the cross. At times he may have thought it better to smooth over such a message. But he could not, for the "word of the cross" was the heart of the gospel. It was the spearhead on the spear and could not be broken off without rendering the spear ineffective.

Today among Churches of Christ the spearhead is sometimes blunt and, in some cases, broken off. We face, therefore, a challenge of the utmost urgency. We face the challenge of letting the cross stand at the center of all our preaching and teaching, and thus becoming a community of the cross. We must see, as Paul saw so clearly, that Christ's cross and resurrection provide the central model for the Christian's life. For Paul, the dying and rising of Christ was not simply something that happened once *for us*, but rather something that must happen daily *within us*.

The life of each Christian becomes a proclamation of the gospel, for he is "always being given up to death for Jesus' sake, so that the life of Jesus may be manifested" (2 Cor. 4:11; cf. 3:10).

Paul puts it pointedly and profoundly in Galatians 6:14: "Far be it from me to glory except in the cross of our Lord Jesus Christ, by which the world has been crucified to me, and I to the world." Here are three crucifixions: the crucifixion of Christ, of the world, and of the self. Each one has enormous implications for Christian living today. Only as we explore those implications and begin to embody them will we ever recover our way. For, whatever else the church may be, it is first and foremost a community of the cross.

In addition to a renewed focus on the cross and on what that means for the Christian life, our response to the secularization of the church must include a new openness to the power of the Holy Spirit. We must recapture the conviction, so central to the people of God throughout the ages, that God is present and active in this world, the conviction that the controlling forces of earth are not mechanical or technological but spiritual. We must learn to speak without embarrassment of God's power at work within us, a "power made perfect in weakness" (2 Cor. 12:9). We must learn to speak of God's Spirit at work in our world and of the church as a fellowship created by the Spirit.

But here, once again, our theological tradition may present obstacles. As we have seen, the Enlightenment with its rationalizing of faith, its banishment of mystery, and its drive for human control of the world, profoundly shaped the perspective of the Restoration Movement. The effect on the doctrine of the Holy Spirit was striking. The Spirit's presence in the world was in effect reduced to words, nothing more. Thus, to be filled with the Spirit meant little more than pondering or memorizing passages of Scripture. The empowerment of the Spirit was little more than the ability to marshall logical and convincing arguments from the Bible.

Today we must see such a view for what it is—a doctrine shaped more by modern rationalism than biblical revelation. We must see such a view as a doctrinal aberration out of step with biblical Christianity and as a serious compromise with the secular spirit of our own age. For its effect is to push God out of our realm and to leave us, in all our weakness, dependent on human initiative and achievement. Its effect, in short, is to secularize the gospel.

But this traditional view runs deep among our people. And when this view is overlaid with the modern spirit of self-reliance and self-help, we may have a difficult time hearing the biblical message. But this is the challenge we face today: the challenge to let go of our own bootstraps, to quench the passion to control our own destinies, to expose the self-help gospel for the heresy it is, and to let God do his work among us.

Here especially we must let Scripture guide us. We must see first the close connection between Christ's cross and resurrection and the power of the Spirit. Paul, for example, does not discuss the Spirit in abstract doctrinal terms; rather, he speaks of the Spirit in the setting of Christ's saving work. Through his cross and resurrection, Christ inaugurated a new age, bringing atonement with God, a new and joyous life, and the hope of resurrection. Christ is the Lord of this new age, and that lordship is executed and extended by the Spirit. Those who are "in Christ," Paul says, are ruled by the Spirit, live according to the Spirit, set their minds on the Spirit (Rom. 8:5ff), and in fact have the Spirit dwelling within them (8:9–11; 1 Cor. 3:16). The Spirit is the resurrected and ascended Christ at work within us.

Throughout Scripture, in both Old and New Testaments, the Spirit is always God at work "down here." The Spirit is God on the move in his world, creating, sustaining, redeeming, purifying. Job declares, "If he should take back his spirit to himself, and gather to himself his breath, all flesh would perish together, and man would return to dust" (Job 34:14–15; cf. Ps. 104:29). Through the prophets, God assures us, "I will put my Spirit within you, and you shall live" (Ezek. 37:11). When God is present in the cities and on the plains of earth, he is there as Spirit. Thus David asks, "Whither shall I flee from Thy Spirit; whither shall I go from Thy presence" (Ps. 139:7).

Paul speaks of the Spirit in remarkably similiar ways, though for him the Old Testament's "Spirit of God" has become the "Spirit of Christ." The Spirit is Christ at work in the world, bringing life to spiritually dead people (2 Cor. 3:6). The presence of the Spirit brings love into our lives, provides confidence, and accounts for the virtues we display (Rom. 5:5; Gal. 5:22–26). It is the indwelling Spirit who enlightens our minds to the things of God (1 Cor. 2:12), who assures our spirits that we are the children of God (Rom. 8:16), and who guarantees our future life with God (Eph. 1:14; 2 Cor. 5:5). Everywhere throughout Scripture the power ascribed to the Spirit is the power to give life.

Further, it is the Spirit who creates, guides, and sustains the church. "For by one Spirit," Paul says, "we were all baptized into one body—Jews or Greeks, slaves or free—and all were made to drink of one Spirit" (1 Cor. 12:13). In Acts, Luke points to the guidance of the Spirit at crucial points in the church's early history: at Pentecost (2:1ff), at the death of Stephen (7:55), at the baptism of the first Gentile (10:44), at the beginning of the first overseas mission (13:2), at the admission of Gentiles without circumcision (15:28), and at the bringing of the gospel to Europe (16:6–10). And it is the Spirit who distributes various gifts and ministries for the building up of the church (1 Cor. 12–14).

For this reason, the earliest Christians believed themselves to be living in the "fellowship of the Spirit" or, more accurately, in "fellowship which the Spirit bestows" (2 Cor. 13:14). The church, they knew, was not their own work; it grew and flourished through the power of the Spirit.

Today we need this same openness to the Spirit as we face the continuing secularization of the church. However awkward it might seem, we need to sing again the words of Luther's great hymn:

Come, Holy Spirit, God and Lord!
Be all Thy graces now outpoured
On the believer's mind and soul,
To strengthen, save, and make us whole.[3]

In addition to a new openness to the Spirit, our response to the secularization of the church will mean a new clarity about Christian worship. Perhaps no single area of modern church life is as confused as this one. Recovering a Word-centered or biblical faith, therefore, will mean recovering the meaning of Christian worship.

Many Christians, correctly concluding that worship does not consist merely in the performance of five specific acts of worship, nonetheless have no clear understanding of what Christian worship ought to be. Misunderstandings range widely. Some would reduce worship to "fellowship," while others try to promote strange emotional experiences. Not surprisingly, in a therapeutic society increasingly occupied with self and "meaningful relationships," "renewed worship" all too frequently incorporates large doses of self-enhancement ("meets *my* needs," "makes *me* feel good"), simple conviviality, and entertainment.

Biblical worship, in contrast, must remove self from the center of concern. It does this through two closely related but separable movements.

First, true worship confronts our ever-expanding egos with the reality of God. It involves a stepping back from our preoccupations with ourselves and our world. As Abram before the smoking pot (Gen. 15), Moses before the burning bush (Ex. 3), and Isaiah in the Temple (Isa. 6), worship involves the overwhelming, dread-inspiring recognition of the Lord of Hosts, the Holy One of Israel—the Transcendent One.

This movement within worship evokes awe, mystery, and reverence. For the Christian, however, it culminates in the recognition that this Transcendent One—Maker and Ruler of the Universe—has ruptured history in the incarnation and disclosed himself in the cross and resurrection of Jesus. Thus to mystery and awe are added gratitude and hope.

Appropriate symbols for this movement of worship are the bowed head, the bent knee, and the contrite but grateful heart.

Second, true Christian worship impels us to serve our neighbors, both near and distant. It entails a "return" to the world of the ordinary. This ordinary world, however, is recommissioned as God's world. It is a world where all who have bowed before the Lord of Hosts, received his care, and acknowledged his claim on their lives now view family, work, and recreation in a new light. True worship both enjoins and equips Christians to reflect God's righteousness, compassion, and justice—both in the church and in the world.

Appropriate symbols for this movement of worship are the basin, the towel, and the outstretched hand.

For Christians to fail properly to distinguish these two basic movements of worship, or simply to collapse worship into distortions of one or the other, seriously cripples the church and damages Christian lives. If we are to recover our way, such a recovery will require a better grasp of the meaning and practice of worship. It will entail our becoming a worshiping community.

Finally, if we are to resist the inroads of secularization, we must allow the power of God to make of us a holy people. The notion of holiness points to sanctification, to separation from the values of the world, and to a firm allegiance to the scandal of the cross.

We spoke earlier of the widespread reverence in our modern world for power, control, and wealth, and in this context especially the Saviour's call to holiness must be heard. We are not called to share the values of power, dominion, and control. Rather, as he submitted to the cross, giving his life for sinners, so he calls us to empty ourselves on behalf of those who have no claim to this world or its goods and no share in its power.

All Scripture attests to a God who works in unexpected ways, who often reverses the human order of things, who draws strength from weakness, blessings from poverty, and from servanthood brings a power that transcends completely the poor, crass expressions of human manipulation and strength. Mary's song puts it simply:

> *He has put down the mighty from their*
> *thrones and exalted those of low degree;*
> *he has filled the hungry with good things,*
> *and the rich he has sent empty away.*
> *(Lk. 1:46–53)*

Mary's song points to a central biblical theme: the God of Abraham, Isaac, and Jacob is a God who regularly acts in history to exalt the weak, the poor, and the oppressed, and to cast down the strong, the rich, and the oppressive.

One of the most pointed declarations of God's passion for the poor and the weak in the Old Testament is Psalm 146. In fact, we learn here that compassion for the weak is central to the very nature of God.

> *Happy is he whose help is the God of Jacob,*
> *whose hope is in the Lord his God,*
> *who made heaven and earth,*
> *the sea, and all that is in them;*
> *who keeps faith forever;*
> *who executes justice for the oppressed;*
> *who gives food to the hungry.*
> *The Lord sets the prisoners free;*
> *the Lord opens the eyes of the blind.*
> *The Lord lifts up those who are bowed down;*
> *the Lord loves the righteous.*
> *The Lord watches over the sojourners,*
> *he upholds the widow and the fatherless;*
> *but the way of the wicked he brings to ruin.*
> *(vss. 1, 5–9)*

This psalm teaches that it is just as much a part of God's nature to defend the weak, the stranger, and the oppressed as it is to create the universe. God lifts up the mistreated, simply because it is his nature to do so.

Then, there are the resounding words of Jesus as he read from Isaiah 61 while in the Nazareth synagogue:

> *The Spirit of the Lord is upon me,*
> *because he has annointed me to preach good*
> *news to the poor. He has sent me to proclaim*
> *release to the captives and recovery of sight to*
> *the blind, to set at liberty those who are op-*
> *pressed, to proclaim the acceptable year of the*
> *Lord. (Lk. 4:18–19)*

After reading these words, Jesus announced to the audience that this Scripture was now fulfilled in himself. The mission of the Incarnate One was to proclaim good news to the poor and free the oppressed.

But there is far more. Not only does God act in history on behalf of the weak and the outcast, but, most astounding of all, God identifies with them. Indeed, the scandal of the cross is precisely the fact that God freely chooses to suffer with and for the suffering people of the earth and to participate in the poverty and the frailty of humankind. Indeed, he shares our life with us. Far from remaining aloof and untouched, he humbles himself and makes himself vulnerable to human beings in all their weakness.

God's identification with the weak, the poor, and the sinful reaches its climax in the incarnation of his Son. Of Jesus, Paul writes, "Though he was rich, yet for your sake he became poor" (2 Cor. 8:9) and "emptied himself, taking the form of a servant, being born in the likeness of men" (Phil. 2:7). Here, we see most clearly how God regards the poor and weak and oppressed of this earth, for his own dear Son became one of them.

It is difficult for us to remember that God is a God of the poor, the weak, and the oppressed. For we tend to form images of God and Christ quite in keeping with the values we prize and the traits we admire. If we admire power and control and prestige, so will our Jesus. If we look down upon weakness of all sorts, so will our Jesus. If we cannot bear to face our own humanness and frailties, we will have a hard time perceiving the humanity of Jesus. And if we have insulated ourselves from the poor and despised of this world, our Jesus will seem aloof from them, too.

But we are called not to make Jesus over in the image of our values, but to allow God to make our values over in the image of his own dear Son. One of the striking aspects of the early years of the Restoration Movement was the great extent to which so many of its leaders understood this call to holiness and separation from the world and lent themselves to God to be remade in his image on behalf of the suffering, the oppressed, and the poor.

Exemplary in this regard was Barton W. Stone whose life was typified by Romans 12:2: "Be not conformed to this world, but be transformed by the renewal of your mind . . . ." Stone urged the "Christians in the West"

> *to be willing to decrease, that Christ may increase—to be willing for truth's sake, to be rejected by all, even to be excluded from the society, with which we may be associated, however popular and respectable it may be....
> [and to] be willing to give up all worldly gain or wealth, for the sake of truth.*[4]

Repeatedly, he admonished his brothers and sisters to care for the widow and the orphan, to minister to the poor and the hungry, to avoid extravagance in dress, and to love one another with pure hearts fervently.[5] For Barton Stone, the restoration of primitive Christianity meant, in large measure, to allow one's life to be transformed by the scandal of the cross.

Another pioneer notable in this regard was Joseph Thomas, often known as the "White Pilgrim." This fascinating man rejected the fashions of the world and embraced a simple, primitive lifestyle for himself. He sold his farm and his horse and rid himself of the garb that was fashionable for preachers of his day. He then donned a long, white robe which he wore for the rest of his life—a symbol of his rejection of the values of the world and of his commitment to his first and only priority, the proclamation of the scandal of the cross. Eccentric to be sure, this man nonetheless committed himself to transcendent values and humble service and soon became known within and without the Restoration Movement for the depth of his conviction.[6]

No wonder that W. D. Jourdan, one of the earliest pioneer preachers, recalled in the twilight of his life that preachers in those days

> *had no bread and butter to lose by preaching against sin in the church or out of it. . . . They insisted that the religion of the Bible was not intended to be mixed up with things of the world, but to be kept separate from all such things in order to maintain its purity in the hearts and actions of men.[7]*

By the 1830s and 1840s, the passion in our movement for holy living and separation from the world already was eroding badly. But one who kept very much alive the vision of a holy church, separate from the world and responsive to the cries of the poor, was David Lipscomb, perhaps the most influential single person among Churches of Christ during the last half of the nineteenth century. Indeed, Lipscomb understood well the scandal of the cross and sought to convey its meaning to his brothers and sisters. Thus, when urged to adapt the work of the church to a business-like model, Lipscomb was quick to contrast the worldly-wise methods of efficient business with the scandal of the cross.

> *Business men.... would not have chosen the infamy of the Cross, and the degradation of the grave.... This is so unbusiness-like that, business men, entering in strive to change it to a more business-like manner.... [But] God's ways are not man's ways...and the foolishness of God is wiser than man.[8]*

It is little wonder, then, that Lipscomb viewed "the poor of this world" as "God's elect," and the church as "the especial legacy of God to the poor of the earth. . . ."[9]

This is all to say that if we in Churches of Christ would take seriously the biblical call to holy, sanctified living, we have rich resources not only in Scripture, but also in the history of our own movement. But most of all, our richest resource is the God who alone can empower us with his Spirit to live out the scandal of the cross in our time.

The God We Proclaim

Many people will remember the story of Corrie ten Boom. As the Nazis swept across Europe in World War II, Corrie and her family began hiding Jews in their native Holland. Eventually the family was arrested and placed in a concentration camp, and there Corrie saw her father and her sister die.

After the war, Corrie ten Boom became a refugee across Europe, trying to bring healing to that broken continent. In her book, *The Hiding Place*, she recounted one particularly striking experience.

> *It was at a church service in Munich that I saw him, the former S.S. man who had stood guard at the shower room door in the processing center at Ravensbruck. He was the first of our actual jailers that I had seen since that time. And suddenly it was all there—the roomful of mocking men, the heaps of clothing, Betsie's pain-blanched face.*
>
> *He came up to me as the church was emptying, beaming and bowing. "How grateful I am for your message, Fraulein," he said. "To think that, as you say, He has washed my sins away!"*
>
> *His hand was thrust out to shake mine. And I, who had preached so often to the people at Bloemendaal the need to forgive, kept my hand at my side.*

*Even as the angry, vengeful thoughts boiled
through me, I saw the sin of them. Jesus Christ
had died for this man; was I going to ask for
more? Lord Jesus, I prayed, forgive me and
help me to forgive him.*

*I tried to smile, and I struggled to raise my
hand. I could not. I felt nothing, not the
slightest spark of warmth or charity. And so
again I breathed a silent prayer. Jesus,
I cannot forgive him. Give me Your forgiveness.*

*As I took his hand the most incredible thing
happened. From my shoulder along my arm
and through my hand a current seemed to
pass from me to him, while into my heart
sprang a love for this stranger that almost
overwhelmed me.*

*And so I discovered that it is not on our for-
giveness any more than on our goodness that
the world's healing hinges, but on His. When
he tells us to love our enemies, He gives,
along with the command, the love itself.*[10]

Here is the God we proclaim, the God who
shatters our little illusions of self-sufficiency and who,
in their place, gives us his power. If we are to be for-
given, comforted, and sustained in this life, our God
will be the one to do it, for there is no one else in all
the world with love enough and power enough to do
so.

He will be the one to pierce our pride, our
pretensions, our smug, hollow goodness, and to chip
away at the idols in our hearts.

He will be the one to wean us from our
frantic quest for happiness and success and from the
ever-multiplying "needs" that keep us enslaved to
things.

He will be the one who comes to us in the burning moments of our lives and who calls us by our names and offers himself to us.

He will be the one to make us holy and compassionate, to nurture in our hearts a love that we could never generate for ourselves.

He will be the one to plant in our hearts that great, deep hope that down through the ages has sustained all the weary people of God.

Our God will be the one to do all these things—things we could never do for ourselves. For he is the one who has opened the heavens and come down to us in his Spirit and in his Son. And from those opened heavens, he is the one who raised Jesus from the dead and who, by that same power, raises us to newness of life.

That new life is not the life that our world seeks or offers—not a life of pomp and show, power and glory, or sensual gratifications. Neither is it the kind of spiritual life that we see promoted today—a life filled with signs and wonders, unceasing light, and constant exuberance. For there is always before us the offense of the cross. There is always before us a suffering God, a God who chose the way of the cross.

That way is always before us. Our God summons us into that way, a way that he himself has taken. That summons is never a summons to celebrate human potential, but always a call to cross-bearing and self-forgetfulness.

Together we follow that way, sometimes with fear and trembling, often by fits and starts, most often looking weak and foolish in the eyes of this world. But we seek to follow at all costs, knowing that the suffering and sovereign God has promised to begin working in our small and reluctant hearts.

Only by heeding that summons will we recover our way.

[1]For a helpful introduction to the discipline of biblical theology, see James D. Smart, *The Past, Present, and Future of Biblical Theology* (Philadelphia: Westminster, 1978).

[2]Martin Hengel, *Crucifixion in the Ancient World and the Folly of the Message of the Cross* (Philadelphia: Fortress, 1977), p. 89.

[3]In *Great Songs of the Church, Revised* (Abilene: Abilene Christian University, 1986).

[4]Barton W. Stone, *Christian Messenger* 1 (November 25, 1826):3.

[5]Stone, "Mourning Apparel," from the *Christian Register*, in *Christian Messenger* 10 (September 1836):136; Stone, et.al., "The Brethren Appointed for that Purpose Report the Following Address," *Christian Messenger* 9 (July 1835):148–149. See also Stone, "The Opinion of the Apostle Peter Respecting Trifles," *Christian Messenger* 12 (July 1842):279–82.

[6]Joseph Thomas, *The Life of the Pilgrim Joseph Thomas* (Winchester, VA, 1818), pp. 253–264.

[7]*American Christian Review* (December 7, 1882).

[8]David Lipscomb, "Discussion—Missionary Societies," *Gospel Advocate* 9 (March 14, 1867):208.

[9]Lipscomb, "New Publications," *Gospel Advocate* 8 (January 1, 1866):11–12; and ibid. (February 27, 1866):141.

[10]Corrie ten Boom, *The Hiding Place* (Washington Depot, CT: Chosen Books, 1971), p. 215.

Conclusion 6

In the preceding pages we have sought to address the basic question of our identity today as a people of God. We have asked "Where are the Churches of Christ today?" "Who are we as a people?" and "What forces are shaping our basic identity?"

We have asked these questions out of deep concern. For the secular forces rampant in our culture have so altered our identity that we now face an "identity crisis" of considerable proportions.

To face the urgent question of our identity today, we have looked in two directions. First, we have looked at the phenomenon of secularization and at how it has worked in our heritage. Second, we have looked again to Scripture, issuing a call to reclaim and herald its central themes.

We can summarize our analysis of secularization with the following points:

*(1) Secularization is one of the basic features
of modern western culture.* A cultural force rooted in
the Enlightenment of the seventeenth and eighteenth
centuries, secularization means the erosion of the
sense of transcendence. As a society becomes secularized, supernatural explanations increasingly give way
to natural ones. In the last one hundred years, the
rapid advance of technology has accelerated the process, leading to a radically this-worldly outlook.

*(2) Secularization has profoundly affected
American Christianity, leading to the emergence of
what we have termed "the secular church."* The secular
church adopts "utility" or "marketability" as its guiding principle. In the process the church alters its identity, function, and message. Rather than stand apart
from the culture, challenging its values, the church
seeks to accommodate the culture, sanctifying many
of its values. Human values and needs tend to replace
biblical revelation as the reference point for its teaching and preaching.

*(3) The secular spirit that has shaped a large
segment of American Christianity is also reshaping the
Churches of Christ.* Though members of Churches of
Christ have imagined themselves to be nothing more
than first-century Christians, they are, in fact, very
much people of the twentieth century, partaking of
the secular assumptions embedded in our culture. We
have changed dramatically in the last fifty years. Once
poor and ill at ease in this world, we have become a
people all too much at home in the world, enjoying its
wealth, preferments, and distractions. And our
churches have kept pace, steadily taking on the con-
tours of the secular culture around us.

*(4) The history of Churches of Christ in
America makes them particularly susceptible to the forces
of secularization.* The crucial fact in this regard is that
the most influential early leaders of the movement
drew heavily upon the thought of the Enlightenment—the very current that propelled the forces of

secularization in the eighteenth century. The result was a rationalization of faith and a spirit of self-reliance that has marked the Churches of Christ ever since.

(5) The Churches of Christ felt the influence of the Enlightenment particularly in their way of reading the Bible and in their view of the Holy Spirit. Under such influence, the Bible became for many a compendium of doctrinal "facts" ready to be arranged into a code of laws or a rigid blueprint. And the Spirit's presence in the world was reduced to little more than the written words of the Bible.

(6) The impact of secularization among Churches of Christ appears today in three trends: the emergence of a prudential gospel, the turn to the self, and the veneration of wealth and status. For many the gospel of Christ has become a mere means to an end, that end being the enhancement and gratification of self. With this turn to the self, Christians find it increasingly difficult to heed Christ's call to commitment, sacrifice, and suffering servanthood.

(7) With the adoption of secular fads and the rush to meet an ever-expanding array of "needs," Churches of Christ are losing their biblical base and becoming confused about what human beings really need. A secular culture constantly generates new "needs," many of them false or secondary. The church that sets its agenda primarily by a market analysis of "needs" will quickly lose its way. It will be unable to expose false "needs" or identify the penultimate "needs" disguised as ultimate ones. Only a constant recourse to Scripture will enable us to meet the ultimate needs to which the gospel speaks.

The identity crisis among Churches of Christ today can be resolved only as we place Scripture at the center of our life together and grapple anew with its message. This will mean, we have suggested, at least the following things.

(1) It will mean a renewal of biblical theology. We must focus our eyes on the great, overarching themes of Scripture and make those themes central in the preaching and teaching of the church. We must herald the majesty and sovereignty of God, the staggering fact of human sin, the unfathomable love of the Father, the death and resurrection of the Son, salvation by grace, and the transforming power of the Spirit. This message will expose the spurious and self-serving "needs" generated by a secular culture and, at the same time, meet the needs that lie at the very center of our being.

(2) It will mean a renewal of authentic Christian ministry. We must learn, first, to take seriously the pervasive dimensions of sin and to admit, in that regard, that all our methods and techniques are poor tools, at best, which address only symptoms, not the disease. If we want to do a Christian work, we must learn to hear the ultimate need behind every temporal need, the final anxiety behind the anxiety of every particular moment, and the ultimate question that haunts all the particular questions that seem so urgent in a given time. And having heard, we must then proclaim the Ultimate Answer which all women and men, in whatever straits or circumstances, need to hear.

(3) It will mean learning to become a community of the cross. We must question the vaunted triumphalism of our time with its focus on power as the means to success. We must learn, instead, to prize humble service, compassion, sacrifice, and uncalculating selflessness, ideals that find little commendation in the secular success manuals.

(4) It will mean a new openness to the power of God's Spirit in our churches. We must put behind us a secularized doctrine of the Spirit, proclaiming instead that God, through his Spirit, is present and active in this world, that he is at work sustaining, redeeming, and transforming his creation. And we must

catch a vision of the church as a people living in the "fellowship of the Spirit."

(5) It will mean a new clarity about Christian worship. We must see in biblical worship two basic dimensions: first, a removal of self from the center of concern and a confrontation with the reality of a transcendent God; and second, a refocusing on the world of the ordinary, where we are enabled to see this world more and more in the light of God's holiness and compassion.

(6) It will mean a renewed passion to live out the biblical vision of the holy life. We must sound the call—as did Barton Stone, David Lipscomb, and others of our spiritual ancestors—to a life separate and apart from worldly values and responsive to the cries of the poor and weak. In the process, we should find our greatest struggles to be not so much with worldly frustrations as with worldly aspirations.

The vision we seek to hold up before Churches of Christ was captured in Shirley Nelson's recent novel, *The Last Year of the War.* The story takes place on the campus of a conservative Bible college during the closing years of World War II. In the daily chapel service one morning, Dr. Peckham, one of the professors, delivered a short talk.

People often ask, he began, about something called the "victorious life" or the "life that wins." Many had asked him if he believed in such a life. Yes, he said, he did, but if he had to give it a name he would rather call it "the life that loses."

He began to explain.

We want to be like Christ, we say. We want to have His heart . . . to be courageous, serene in the face of adversity, powerful in soul-winning, steady and unmovable in faith, free from the tyranny of self, flesh crucified, all in our places, with sunshiny faces.

*But friends, it may not be that way. If you ask
for the heart of Christ, yours may be broken. If
you ask for the eyes of Christ, you may be
horrified at what you see. If you try to embrace
all mankind, as Christ did, you may be con-
sumed by that love. Touching broken lives
means to be touched back by the world's mis-
ery. The healer risks infection. The diseases are
fear, loneliness, even insanity. If we fight in-
justice, we are identified with the condemned.
We will bear about in our bodies the paradoxes of mankind, the yeas and the nays.*

*To be a Christian in the truest sense may
mean to live on the edge of a cliff, shocked and
dismayed at our own weaknesses, failure and
evil. We go there as pilgrims and pioneers, and
only God can keep us safe on that wild fron-
tier.*[1]

Here is the central paradox of the gospel.
Paul, reflecting back upon his own life, put it sharply:
"We are treated as imposters, and yet are true; . . . as
dying, and behold we live; as punished, and yet not
killed; as sorrowful, yet always rejoicing; as poor, yet
making many rich; as having nothing, and yet possessing everything" (2 Cor. 6:8–10).

And Jesus said, "If any man would come
after me, let him deny himself and take up his cross
daily and follow me. For whoever would save his life
will lose it; and whoever loses his life for my sake, he
will save it" (Lk. 9:23–24).

Only as we take these words to heart will we
find our true identity as an authentic people of God.

Notes   [1]Shirley Nelson, *The Last Year of the War* (New York:
Harper & Row, 1978), pp. 202–203.

For Further Reading

Barth, Karl. *The Word of God and the Word of Man.* New York: Harper & Brothers, 1958.

Bellah, Robert N., et. al. *Habits of the Heart: Individualism and Commitment in American Life.* New York: Harper & Row, 1986.

Berger, Peter. "Toward a Critique of Modernity." In *Facing up to Modernity.* New York: Harper & Row, 1977.

Collins, Gary. *Beyond Easy Believism.* Waco: Word, 1982.

Eller, Vernard. *The Outward Bound: Caravaning as the Style of the Church.* Grand Rapids: Eerdmans, 1975.

_____. *The Simple Life: The Christian Stance Toward Possessions.* Grand Rapids: Eerdmans, 1973.

Ellul, Jacques. *The Subversion of Christianity.* Grand Rapids: Eerdmans, 1986.

Forbes, Cheryl. *The Religion of Power.* Grand Rapids: Zondervan, 1983.

Hunter, James D. *American Evangelicalism: Conservative Religion and the Quandary of Modernity.* New Brunswick: Rutgers, 1983.

Molnar, Thomas. *The Pagan Temptation: How Rationalistic Christianity Paves the Way for Paganism.* Grand Rapids: Eerdmans, 1987.

Myers, David G. *The Inflated Self: Human Illusions and the Biblical Call to Hope.* New York: Seabury, 1980.

Newbigin, Lesslie. *Foolishness to the Greeks: The Gospel and Western Culture.* Grand Rapids: Eerdmans, 1986.

Postman, Neil. *Amusing Ourselves to Death: Public Discourse in an Age of Entertainment.* New York: Anchor/Doubleday, 1985.

Saliers, Don E. *Worship and Spirituality.* Philadelphia: Westminster, 1984.

Turner, James. "Enlightenment and Belief, 1690–1790." In *Without God, Without Creed: The Origins of Unbelief in America.* Baltimore: Johns Hopkins, 1985.

Voskuil, Dennis. *Mountains into Goldmines: Robert Schuller and the Gospel of Success.* Grand Rapids: Eerdmans, 1983.

Walters, Tony. *Need, the New Religion: Exposing the Language of Need.* Downers Grove: InterVarsity, 1985.